RICHARD HILL

HOW THE
'real world'
IS DRIVING US
CRAZY!

Solving the
WINNER/LOSER WORLD
Problem

Hill & Hill p/l
publishers

Visit the website:
www.creativeworldway.com
Send an email, join the forum –
participate and engage!

Hill & Hill p/l publishers
PO Box 124, Gordon NSW 2072
First published in 2006

The National Library of Australia Cataloguing-in-Publication data:

Hill, Richard C., 1954-
How the 'real world' is driving us crazy!
Solving the Winner/Loser World Problem
ISBN 0-9580890-1-9 (pbk)
ISBN 0-9580890-2-7 (cdrom)
1.Happiness 2.Self-realization 3. Interpersonal relationships.
I. Title   158.1

Cover design by Andy Gibson and Richard Hill
Typeset by Hill & Hill p/l in Garamond
Printed in Australia by Griffin Press

*This book is the outcome of a long
conversation that has continued
throughout my life. I dedicate this book
to all those people who lent me their ear,
those ears that I hijacked and even those
who wished they could have gotten away.
Also, to the great minds that responded,
shared and inspired me.*

*Most of all to John, who began this conversation
with a desktop calendar when I was 8 years old.
He left too soon.*

CONTENTS

♦♦♦ PREFACE ♦♦♦

For many years I have wondered why people need so much help to feel good about themselves and their lives. I was in my twenties when motivational seminars and self-help books began to take off. I remember a friend taking me to EST; I was around the people who were introducing Deepak Chopra, Stuart Wilde and Wayne Grady to Australia; and watching the square-jawed, fast-talking Anthony Robbins on late-night television, urging us to 'release the giant within'.

My personal journey has included acting, singing, business adventures, marriage, children and an inspiring participation in the new age movement. This led to a return to university studies where I achieved a BA in linguistics and later a Diploma in Professional Counselling. I saw some people make great breakthroughs in their personal happiness and development. I also saw many who didn't. What was most intriguing was the significant number of people who were searching, found something, and then decided they needed more. What they first thought to be a great revelation or answer didn't last, and their search had to begin again.

Two important factors stood out: firstly, that human beings in our modern society find it difficult to be happy; and secondly, that most of the 'how to be happy' programs were unable to satisfy the need to be happy for a prolonged time. Something was making happiness very difficult to understand and maintain. It has been shown that external things, like being praised, achieving a goal or being amused can help you to feel happy, but it doesn't last. Happiness must come from within. This is not to say that there aren't extremely happy and content people. In fact, because there are, that must mean that whatever gets in the way is not insurmountable or unresolvable.

This book is about that interference, the disruption to our ability to 'feel happy'. It is my contribution to everyone that still searches for happiness and personal fulfilment. The difference between this book and others before it is that I am not going to show you another way to lift your emotions, although the book may do that as well. I am not even going to show you a way around the barrier. I am going to show you that there is no barrier – we made it up.

Imagine we are living in a world of water. All the courses, seminars and books teach us how to swim or float, or to build boats or even submarines, but they are all skills and techniques that only give us an advantage in the world of water. What is really driving us crazy, however, is that we can't stand being wet. By getting out of the water and onto the shore then our watery problems are more than solved: they cease to exist.

That is what you can expect as you work through this book. First, I have to describe to you what the water world is all about and then what it is like to be on the shore. The task for you is to try and accept that these shores exist when all you've ever known is the water. This is even more so for those that have made some success of living in the water, despite any struggle with happiness.

As I said, I believe that there are people who have found the shore and many others who have been there for a period, but have eventually slipped back into the water. They will be our living guides and helpers.

A lot of experiences and people have gone into the development of this book. My mother, Deirdre O'Donnell, an author of some note herself, has supported me, listened to me and strengthened my heart for as long as I can remember. She has shown me how to write, use grammar and get the spelling right. Her influence is on every page.

My children, Jessica and Joel are huge fonts of inspiration and support. Jessica's creative talent and Joel's computer genius have given me more than I imagined possible. Their mother and my partner for 20 years, Lynda, was a great person to begin my journey with. Also with me during the last 20 years has been my good friend Garry Wiseman, who has provided not only friendship, but also audiences for me to speak to. The inspiration for this work belongs to those thousands of people that shared their lives with me.

This book is a symbol of my new journey, which has been made into an extraordinary experience by my partner and wife, Sue Davis. She has helped me bring my ideas to life. At 6.05am most mornings I begin sharing what is going through my head, and that might well continue all day. She is a wonder.

I also want to thank her son Peter, who was willing to be a guinea pig, along with Jessica and Joel, for my ideas. My sister-in-law Cheryl has been a patient patient. There are also a number of my children's friends who have lent their youthful ears. Special thanks to Lucy who listened and discussed, and also to Aaron, Isaac, Annie, Loretta, Carly and Kelly. Thanks also to Andy, who devoted his creative time to designing the cover of this book. At Sue's clinic, The Davis Health Centre, I thank my other readers and listeners, Sue and Michael, Roy, Dionne and Roger, John, Garry and all my wonderful clients who have tried and tested the techniques.

Last, but by no means least, I would like to thank Dr Daniel Siegel, Dr Ernest Rossi and Dr William Glasser for their intellectual contribution. When I first listened to Daniel Siegel I found myself listening to the intellectual evidence for almost all of my ideas, philosophies and theories. His work has allowed me to proceed directly to the production of this book without having to spend several more years finding the evidence. Daniel Siegel's work on 'mindsight' and Ernest Rossi's work on genomic expression and brain plasticity are intellectual masterpieces, as well as being creative and inspirational jewels. Dr Glasser's work, which includes Reality Therapy and Choice

Therapy, has provided a resonance that has propelled me forward. Jean Houston champions an extraordinary process that she calls Social Atistry. Her work to revitalise the joy of culture and heritage around the world has been a great inspiration to me. I urge you to seek out their work.

It won't take you long to realise that there is always more to know, so I want to thank you in advance for all the comments and suggestions, contributions and thoughts you send through the website and other media. Join me at www.creativeworldway.com and let's see what amazing things happen.

SECTION 1

THE WAY OF THE WORLDS

♦♦♦ A VERY PERSONAL ACCOUNT ♦♦♦

Wherever there is a conscious mind, there is a point of view.
Daniel Dennett

I have spent a number of years watching and participating in self-development programs. I always wondered why, for a lot of people, they don't seem to work for very long. After all these years, I find that the number of people searching for something to give them greater happiness has increased, not decreased.

As a professional counsellor much of my work involves helping clients understand why they believe that their lives are a mess. Therapies help, but they don't change the fact that something is amiss with what we believe the world is all about and what the struggle is for. This has been my consuming investigation for the last decade. I was fortunate to have my first book *Choose Hope* (HarperCollins) published in 2000. Those ideas have grown into this book.

I believe my ideas are fresh and add some illumination, but there are many pointers and clues in other work. The foundations were solidly set by the work of Edward De Bono and he continues to broach new territory. Still, no one that I can find has given the problem a simple explanation.

We live in a social system that is based on separate individuals in a competitive environment. The problem with this is that we are an interactive species that prefers relationship and communal co-operation. Many motivational and self-help programs try to show how it is possible to be loving and feel connected. These programs try to show you how to get 'in touch with yourself' or open up your 'sensitive side', but neglect to give you a clear understanding of why you are not loving and why you feel disconnected. Equally, there are the other programs that show you how to ditch the sensitive caring stuff and just win at all costs.

Maintaining a loving and connected life is constantly compromised by the 'success imperative' to do it on your own. When you do go it alone you are constantly touched by the human need to be close to others. We are torn between the need to succeed - to win - and the desire to connect – to share. The constant struggle between these principles is a conflict that is driving us crazy. I say this because the evidence shows it. We are in an upward spiral of stress and anxiety that is making happiness increasingly difficult and depression increasingly common. Relationships, friendships and families are suffering; more and more people are buckling under the stress of the struggle for success; drugs and alcohol are more available and more frequently used to 'get out of it'; prescription anti-depressants are everywhere; and suicide amongst our youth is increasing as they seek to escape the pressures of what many believe to be a pointless future. We need to figure out how to do the things we want to do without falling apart.

That is what you will achieve if you embrace the ideas and the program in this book. It is not just another book trying to cheer you up, or showing you how to 'beat the system'. This book will show you a *different* system. In order to achieve this, however, I need to explain and describe some new things. I also need to create a common language so that we are on the same wavelength. That is what the first part of the book will do.

You might well be asking now, "Hey, I just want to know how this book is going to help me. Give me a good reason to take the time to read it."

The best answer to give you, before the book has had an opportunity to explain anything at all, is to tell you how these ideas and the program have affected *me*. I have been developing and practicing this program for a number of years, during which time I have worked on the principles with my wife and a number of my clients, to great success. In the end, however, how you feel about something is a very subjective thing. So, this is how it feels for me:

I find it extraordinary.

It is not some dreamlike or ethereal other world. I still experience the same environment, but everything is different in the way it affects me. I have not gone to an oasis or another universe. I can stand up amidst the whole unruly cacophony without that feeling of dread or fear that something terrible will happen. Equally, I'm not full of expectation that wonderful things will happen. Everything is possible, all at once.

I don't fear defeat, or failure; there is no more dissatisfaction, no more discontent, no more feeling not good enough (these things do exist temporarily, but they are passing. It is the lingering of these feelings that breaks you down). There is less confusion about what is important in my life. I am less disturbed when criticised; there are no distressing feelings of loss when things change; no more pain about yesterday or dread about tomorrow; no more dissatisfaction with what is happening now; and no more blind following because I'm too stupid to understand.

From this 'new world' I can love with unconditional acceptance and uninhibited passion. I don't have to love everyone, but everyone is included and everyone is accepted – even the people I don't like much, because that is all right, too. I can listen and accept without having to agree or disagree and I can be inspired by everything I encounter. I am able to feel sorrow without losing the ability to be happy. I can struggle through difficulty without suffering or fearing failure. I can allow my emotions to speak to me without fear or embarrassment. I can give the lives of those I love energy and confidence and I can give people I don't even know a sense of connection and communion without doing anything in particular, just being there.

I am happy. My heart is open. I feel no danger. I can participate in my experience, whatever it is. I feel no limitations, only my potential and a future of possibilities. I can release my passions and my mind.

And all this can be done in full awareness and acceptance of everything that exists around me. I am not in a dream, I am crystal clear. I am not ignoring anything in my environment - I embrace it all. I am not pretending to be anything or anyone; I am just being what I am and who I am.

I am not a winner. I am not a loser. I am a creative participant in life.

I am able to love and to be loved. I am irrepressibly happy. And I truly wonder what it will be like for you.

◆ ◆ ◆ ◆ ◆ ◆ ◆ ◆ ◆ ◆

This book is not just another explanation of how to be happy, although I certainly want a great deal of happiness to come out of the process. This book is about the context in which we experience our lives. Perhaps we have focussed too much on what we can be, and given too little attention to what we live in and how that affects what we can be. I know that there are some wonderful books in the marketplace that explain how to be happy and feel fulfilled. I have read many of these books and they tend to make similar conclusions. What *I* have been trying to understand is why, when these steps to a happy life are in so many publications and seem to be so simple and straightforward, we are still *not* happy. We are more than just *not* happy; we are *less* happy and increasingly more depressed. This book is about why it is so difficult to take these basic and straightforward steps to happiness.

Having said that, I think that many of these processes are very useful. I am even assuming that you are already aware of these processes. It is, however, unwise to make assumptions so, below is my summary of the *10 Steps to Happiness* as presented in the many and varied books on the self-help bookshelf. In the right conditions, these steps can create a genuine pathway to happiness. It is the barriers to and distractions from this pathway that I am concerned about. I'm sure you will recognise many things on this list.

10 things to do to live a happier and more fulfilling life:

1. believe in yourself
2. slow down – take time to smell the roses
3. have positive emotions
4. be interested in the best things you do and the best things other people do
5. have good friends
6. have a purpose in life – make plans, set goals
7. live in the moment – be mindful, undisturbed by prejudice and fear
8. take time to talk AND listen
9. be kind to others and let others be kind to you
10. know that you have a right to be happy, that you deserve to be happy

There are lots more, of course: have good health; do satisfying work; hold a strong belief; don't carry your negative feelings with you; don't take out your frustrations on other people, especially loved ones; laugh; make changes for the better; free yourself from money worries; plant something and nurture it. With all these ways to be happy we should be living in a world full of happiness. But we don't.

About 2,300 years ago a wise Greek named Epicurus suggested that happiness was simple. All that was required were three things:

1. friends, in whom one saw a reflection of oneself.
2. to contemplate your actions in order to learn from mistakes.
3. to be free of the State. By the state he meant the governing or ruling institution. He recognised that institutions were unable to act in an individual's interests and had powers that enabled it to interfere with an individual's expression and liberty.

Point 1 and 2 are quite obvious and are reflected in a number of the points in our 'top 10'. Point 3, however, is quite unusual and has a lot of deep implications. For a start, how would you define 'the state' today? Whatever your definition, it will be about the institutional *context* or the social *constructs* in which we live. This book is my answer to that question and what the implications reveal.

I wish I could explain everything in one sentence, but I need more than that. Read on and I'll see you in the 'new world'.

✦✦✦ HOW TO USE THIS BOOK ✦✦✦

The book is presented in three sections. The first section describes and explains the elements of the idea. It's a *how-to* and *what-does-it-all-mean* manual. Most of the information you need to understand and begin to implement this program is found in this first section.

Section 2 is a deeper look at a number of different ideas that explain and example the material in Section 1. I've borrowed the title 'Through the Looking Glass' from Lewis Carroll because it might feel like you are seeing the world from the other side of a mirror. Not that everything is opposite - just different. We will re-examine some of the things we take for granted and some things we never think about at all.

Section 3, For the Geeks, is a short, but enticing burst of imaginative thought about some of the possibilities and thought miracles I have encountered while trying to understand and describe the winner/loser world theory. This is a chapter about possibilities and is designed to act as a springboard to future ideas and knowledge.

Scattered throughout are stories, case examples and parables that highlight the principles and practices described. These will show you how this theory can be implemented on a day-to-day basis, and also to simply provide some entertainment to refresh your thinking processes as you go.

Finally, the Appendix is a set of real-life stories that you can use for discussion, experiment and inspiration.

Enjoy.

◆◆ THE 'REAL WORLD' IS DRIVING ME CRAZY! ◆◆

We are in a time of moral disengagement and it is an epidemic that is growing.

Albert Bandura

"What a day. I tell you, this world is driving me crazy!"

How many times have you heard or said that lately? How many times have you heard or said that today? On any given day there are dozens of things that make life more difficult. At least, that's the way it feels.

The car won't start; the bus is late; there's a spot on your new clothes; the coffee isn't hot enough; the cap won't come off the jar; your toast burns; your partner gets angry about something; you don't have enough toll for the bridge; your boss tells you off; your fellow worker criticises you about something; the kids won't get ready for school; you find it hard to do the things you used to do; there's nowhere to park at the shops; the price of fuel has gone up... and that's just the tip of the iceberg.

On their own these things may not be that much of a bother, but pile them up, one on top of the other, and by mid-morning you can become a frustrated, cranky powder keg. And these are just the simple things. There's also the serious stuff: not enough money for the bills; the kids are sick; parents or grandparents need extra care; school exams or assignments are due; your body is changing; your relationship is in trouble; there's a death; a new school; a new job; you're constantly forgetting things... and that is just the tip of *that* iceberg.

Some days you feel as though you just can't win a trick. With so many things coming at you from so many directions it's a miracle we can find the occasional win at all. It is really no big surprise that we are stressed and anxious and that so many people feel depressed. Certainly *something* is driving us crazy.

Surely, no one *wants* to be stressed or anxious or depressed, but simply living in the 'real world' seems to do just that.

So what is distressing about these difficulties? The distress is that we feel as if these troubles are personal attacks and personal failures. Our inability to cope with these troubles interferes with our ability to enjoy life and achieve our goals. We are *supposed* to cope. Sometimes you feel like a real loser and nothing is going right. This interferes with your efforts to be a success. In the 'real world' you *must* have success if you want to get anywhere.

We all want to be winners and, definitely, no one wants to be a loser. Our struggle to win in the 'real world' often gets us down, and many feel like failures. We can lose our advantage with little or no warning. Why is this a problem? Because winning, being a success, and getting it right in the 'real world' has become a measure of your worth as a person. Good things come to winners; losers are forced to wait for what they want, or even suffer consequences.

I can imagine you asking me another question: "Surely winning and losing is a reality? If two people are running for the finish line and one gets there first then that person is the winner." Of course that is true, but in our society winning means so much more than just crossing the finish line first. It has become an elemental social measure of your personal worth and value. If you lose, the message you get (and often the one you give yourself) is that there is something wrong with *you*. It is very personal. *You* have a problem. *You* are at a disadvantage. You are not good enough. It is all about *you*.

This creates a very strong pressure on you to step up and find some way to get back to a winning position. There is actually a lot of learning that can be gained from winning or losing, but more often than not we become overpowered by the *importance* of winning or losing. Winning brings approval and reward.

Winners make friends and are looked up to. Winners are shown respect and admired. Winners get the money. Winners get the girl or the guy. Winners get the praise. Winners are treated differently. So are losers. They are not good enough, not strong enough, not fast enough, not *anything* enough. Losing certainly motivates you to do better, but that is largely because winning is a much better place to be. Winners need to make the success linger and losers need to make the failure go away.

I speak with many people who cope with their 'loser' feelings by trying to make some sense of it. Some will say they are just having temporary bad luck; others say they feel some stress, but it's not unbearable; and others protest that winning isn't important to them and the stress they feel is just a normal part of living. Still, almost no one denies that these things bother them, and everyone wishes life wasn't like that. Nobody wants to admit to being a loser, even if they are. In fact, *especially* if they are. Insisting that you are not a loser is a typical reaction in a winner/loser world.

Here is a brief collection of things people have told me they do to feel like winners again: buy lottery tickets to help solve the problem of debts, only to find that when they lose they feel worse than before; yell at their wife, husband or children because they've been yelled at by their boss all day; go out of their way to be really nice to everyone, which then leads to feelings of disappointment when people don't acknowledge or return their kindness; criticise others to try and boost their own self-esteem, only to find that when that criticism is returned they end up feeling worse and more insecure; some even lie or brag about how successful/wealthy/capable they are.

We all do these things and more to try and regain some advantage or to get back on top. Why do we do these things? Why do we believe that we *need* to do these things? Why do we not see how unhappy this makes us? To answer this we need a better understanding of this thing called the 'real world'.

♦♦♦ THE REAL WORLD ♦♦♦

The pleasures of the world are deceitful; they promise more than they give. They trouble us in seeking them, they do not satisfy us when possessing them and they make us despair in losing them.

Madame de Lambert

Have you ever said or heard someone say, "Well, that was fun, but now we have to get back to the real world", or when someone talks about their dreams and desires they are told, "That sounds great, but it will never work in the real world"? It seems reasonable to assume from these common colloquial statements that the 'real world' is somewhere you are *supposed* to be and, even though you may be able to enjoy brief escapes when you are on holiday, having fun, or entertaining exciting or innovative ideas, at some point it is necessary to get back to the 'real world'.

So that means, except for brief excursions into some sort of 'unreal world', we have no option other than to live in the 'real world', regardless of what happens or how it makes us feel. Most people believe it is the only world we've got. In fact, it is generally believed that if you can't make it in the 'real world' then you have a serious problem. It is *your* responsibility to make the most of your opportunities and if you fail, that is your misfortune. We believe that the 'real world' presents us with plenty of opportunity to make a success and be a winner. It is up to each individual to make it happen for themselves. Or so we are told.

Yet, there are people who work hard, try hard, give their best and are still told by bosses, friends, family or partners they are not good enough. Far too many people look at their reflection in the mirror and find it unacceptable. How can so many people feel lonely when there are so many of us? I have clients who seek help because they find it easier to be angry about something than happy. Why is the struggle for success so often at the expense of family, relationships and friendships? Too often we find ourselves too busy for others, especially the ones we love. These are just some of the symptoms of an increasingly overpowering winner/loser world. These problems of the 'real world' may begin as a personal issue, but they affect us all and the results are disturbing and dramatic.

At this time we are suffering an unparalleled epidemic of unhappiness that is manifesting as depression, fear, loneliness and other emotional distress. This may not be the case for everyone all the time. You may be coping well in your own situation, but overall, it is affecting our personal lives, our relationships, the enjoyment of our workplace and even our very survival. More and more we hear, talk and read about separation, disconnection and isolation in our communities, our families and our countries. Drug use is becoming more commonplace and the hustle for money is unrelenting. It is, surely, driving us crazy.

In a world built on progress we are progressing toward some very undesirable places. Between 1950 and 1995, Australian suicide rates rose sharply, with a clear increase in the proportion of suicides in the under-45 age group. Suicide rates among 15-24-year-olds tripled. Suicide rose from comprising 6% of premature deaths in 1983 to 9.2% in 1995. In 1995 there were 2,366 suicide deaths in Australia: 1,871 were male (79%), 355 of which were under 25 years of age (19%).

It is not just at this extreme end of the profile that we find an increase in destructive symptoms. Relationships are suffering. Many find it increasingly difficult, and some find it near impossible, to just 'get on' with people around them. Fewer people know their neighbours. Competition at primary school level causes anxiety and stress. Magazines impose the right look or the right weight or the right job or the right way to have sex. Companies are spending big dollars on boosting employee morale to maintain productivity, an expense that is not always effective. Advertisers constantly remind us of how much better our lives would be - if. This is all costing us dollars, but, more importantly, it is costing us our health and happiness - and surely that's costing us dollars, too. Yet, all this is happening in a time of boom. Boom times should be happy times, shouldn't they?

Something is wrong with the things we believe are worth living and working for. Hundreds of therapies and practices are available to help people, both in themselves and their relationships with others. Despite this, stress and anxiety are getting worse. We must look seriously look at some 'sacred cows'. There is a lot of discussion about how things *should* be better, how things *should* change or even that we should just *get away from it all*. But what is this 'all' that we need to get away from and where can we go?

It seems clear that the 'real world', this world where winning and losing is the dominant objective, is what we seek to get away from. If we want more of an 'unreal world' where there is less pressure, where it's easier and more friendly, then we have to work out how that is possible. The dilemma is this: when winning is the goal it is necessary to act, at some stage or other, separately and independently in order to come out 'on top'. Bottom line is that to win, to be first, you have to be on your own, you have to 'look out for No 1'. Paradoxically, there's a mile of literature (and common sense) that tells us human beings need to connect with each other, care for each other and help each other. We suffer when we feel separated or disconnected from people in our community, at work or home. We desire, yearn and search for connection, but the 'winner/loser world' demands, requires and rewards us when we don't. It doesn't seem possible to do both at the same time. This is the *winner/loser world* problem: winning benefits from separation whereas happiness benefits from connection. It seems you can have one or the other. Any struggle to have both creates conflict. The result is that we feel separated and disconnected. Eventually we feel depressed, afraid and lonely.

How does this work? With surprising ease. When under stress or in difficulty it is only natural to enlist support or help. If we do enlist support it just doesn't seem 'right' to be given help for too long. We eventually feel the pressure to disengage and refocus on our individual struggle, which, of course, causes us stress. To alleviate this stress we again seek to engage with others, until we succumb to the pressure of having to 'do it yourself' so we disengage, which affects our feelings of security and sense of love, so we seek to engage to revitalise those lost feelings, but we are then open to the criticism of being emotionally weak and a loser so we disengage to show everyone how tough we are, but this is very emotionally painful and so we seek to engage, but we have already alienated or distanced ourselves from those in our closer circle and we have to look elsewhere. We try to engage with anyone, maybe a stranger or some professional whom tries to help us engage again, but by now we don't even know what being engaged is anymore. When we get to this stage we start to feel like we are going a little crazy. And that is partly true, but not because you are truly crazy. You are torn. You are tired. You are confused. You are in the winner/loser world, and that is what it does to you.

There must be a way of living, some 'other world' that is based on connection and interaction where we can feel good about what we do, who we are, and still be able to achieve something. The trouble with most of the alternative lifestyles is that they don't actually address the central problem. Some involve dropping out or teaching a different definition of success. Some make success synonymous with happiness (remember Gordon Gecko and "greed is good"), whereas others suggest making a sacrifice of success for the reward of personal connection and inner peace. Many people who have tried these alternatives found that when they got an answer they were soon confronted by a new question. Self-esteem has been found and lost over and over again.

No amount of trying to make the 'real world' less of a winner/loser experience or finding ways to help us feel any less of a loser has had any lasting effect, other than to make things worse. You can't make a silk purse out of a sow's ear. The winner/loser world problem is unresolvable from *within* the winner/loser world: you cannot get dry when you are still in the water. This is not something that can be fixed. It is something that must be changed.

We spend so much time and energy feeling frustrated by things that don't seem to make sense or seem hard to understand. "I can't understand why this is happening to me", "I don't know why he isn't affectionate", "I don't understand how they can be so selfish", "It doesn't make any sense for her to feel ugly when she is so special". These are the sorts of things we all hear and shake our heads with puzzlement. But in the context of the winner/loser world, it is easy to understand. This is exactly what we should expect to happen. Just as you can't solve being wet while you stay in the water, the only true solution to the winner/loser world problem is to leave the world where we are so easily disappointed, where men feel uncomfortable to share their emotions, where selfishness is often the preferred option and where we can not only feel ugly, but also have to compensate by being told we are 'special'.

We need a complete shift, one that breaks the ever worsening spiral of stress and anxiety, without having to reject or escape or hide from the so-called 'real world' – just put it in its proper place. It is not possible for everyone to turn their backs on our social structures and systems. It *is* possible, however, to shift the way we measure our personal worth and the way we look at this 'real world' we live in.

The following analogy may help you understand what I mean. An excellent dramatisation of how we can become consumed by a 'world' that we believe to be the only 'real world' is the basis of the film, *The Matrix*. A 'world' was created by the machines to make people feel they were living a 'real life', but they weren't. They just *believed* they were. It was an invention. Some people, like the lead character Neo, sensed that something was wrong, but 'the matrix' was all anybody *could* know – unless they took the red pill. When Neo took the pill he found there was a whole existence that he was unaware of and had been unable to access. When he left 'the matrix' and understood the truth, he was then able to exist in both worlds, entering and leaving 'the matrix' at will.

This book is a 'red pill'.

♦♦♦ SO, WHAT IS THE 'OTHER WORLD'? ♦♦♦

There is no victory in the stuff of life. There is only victory in the love of life, for without the love of life, the stuff of life is not worth fighting for.

Richard Hill

The 'other world' seems obvious: a world of relationships and caring for others; a world of love, kindness and sharing; a world of happiness. If only it were that simple. Being happy in the winner/loser world has proved to be surprisingly and depressingly difficult. It is hard to understand why people will choose conflict over happiness, but that seems to be the case. I no longer believe that that conflict is just a poor choice. I am beginning to see that it is an inevitable and largely unavoidable result of the winner/loser world problem.

The more I look at the 'world' we live in and the way people try to cope with it, the more obvious it seems that the things we do to either win, avoid losing or recover from losing are incompatible with relationship, interaction and connection. The more we try to fix it, the more we amplify the problem. There are many wonderful ideas and programmes and how-to systems that try to help us feel better, but most end up trying to make you feel like a winner of some sort or other.

The last decade or so has focussed heavily on 'personal power'. This has become an important new measure of being a winner, but in many of the people I come across, this has just created more losers. We are no closer to better relationships, happier communities or positive connection by using these methods. They just alter the distribution of power or redefine who is winning.

We are titillated by being told that we can have anything we want; do anything we want; heal anything we want; be anything we want; and find great relationships. We are shown how to create success and fortune by copying the successful and the fortunate. Alternatively we are shown how to connect to greater, mysterious powers that will give us special protection. We are given promises that we can be loved and wanted, and have the freedom to follow our passions and desires. We can discover how to never feel bad about ourselves again. Everyone is searching for some way to be that little bit better and more acceptable, a way to tap into some special advantage. In short – to be winners. I'm not saying that we shouldn't try to improve ourselves and that these programs haven't been helpful in keeping many of us afloat in difficult times, but the statistics show that they haven't worked well enough. They may keep us afloat, but they still leave us trapped in the winner/loser world. Our ability to enjoy a genuine connection with others continues to degenerate.

So, what must we do? Certainly, we must re-examine what we believe, because our beliefs are the foundation of who we are. If the 'real world' is based on separation, which has resulted in a system of winning and losing, then the 'other world' must be based on connection, interaction and relationship. What type of world could come from connection and interaction? What do we look for?

Firstly, it must be something that is founded on a basic element of human behaviour. This behaviour needs to be well developed and natural. Secondly, it must be something that is not restricted to 'special' people or limited by any individual quirk of birth. Thirdly, it has to be something that can take us forward as an individual without forcing us to be separate from others. Lastly, it needs to be something that can produce a helpful and beneficial outcome even in difficult circumstances - and it must do all these things at the same time.

There is one quality of being human that satisfies all these things. This quality is at the centre of the way humans function. It is the spontaneous process that occurs when things come together and interact. It is elemental to everyone, favours no one and is always able to produce a beneficial outcome. This quality is our inner creativity.

Straight away I can imagine some readers are questioning again, 'Isn't creativity about talent, some ability to paint or sing or write?' No - and I emphasise – *absolutely* not. That is *outward creative expression*, which is very different from our inner creative capacity. It may be difficult at first to grasp the nature and importance of our innate creative capacity, but that is because we have been dominated for such a long time by a world where you are measured by what you do and how you do it in a disconnected and separate environment. In the new world, just like Neo in *The Matrix*, we will have to retrain ourselves, learn new systems, understand how the winner/loser world came about and discover the wonders of the new world. I'd like to call this new place the 'Creative World'.

♦♦♦ THE CREATIVE WORLD ♦♦♦

Trying to find the 'right' answer is the problem — there isn't one. However, to respond to life with inspired, creative vigour is the great miracle of being human.

Richard Hill

Our natural creativity is one of the main reasons why human beings have survived as a species. We have evolved on a planet that has gone through a lot of changes. Our advantage has been our capacity to adapt and adapting comes from our ability to create. After the dinosaurs died out mammals continued to evolve, eventually leading to the appearance of man. In the 60 million years since the demise of the dinosaurs, modern human beings (*Homo sapiens*) have only been around for about 150,000 years. We have become the dominant species on the planet incredibly quickly because of our extraordinary capacity to take what is available to us in the present moment and create something more in the next moment. More often than not we will create an improvement that increases our chances of survival and benefits our current well being. This is how a species survives and succeeds.

This tendency to create beneficial improvements is not always done with conscious intervention or intention. In fact, mostly our interactions with the environment are non-conscious. Tending toward a beneficial outcome is the nature of creativity. This will be discussed in more detail in the chapter on harmony (see Section 2).

Without ever consciously knowing it, our body and mind are constantly at work receiving information from our environment. From that information we firstly create awareness that we exist, then where we are in our environment and what is changing as we interact. For example, we see movement in the hallway that attracts our attention. Our eyes receive photons of light that are picked up by receptors in the eye, which send signals to the visual cortex in the brain. This interacts with information from our memory and our emotions, which trigger a host of other mental processes. Our other senses in the form of smell, sound, taste and touch are all involved. Our musculo-skeletal system and nervous system tell us how we are standing or moving; and our emotional centres are monitoring our safety as well as other feelings, like pleasure or satisfaction. We gather all the information that is available, and these interact to create responses that seek to produce the best outcome. This integrated creative process is happening continuously, and often in the time-space of milliseconds. We recognise the family cat, smile and pick it up for a comforting tummy rub.

The processes above could be a description of any number of things in your life. It could be when you are playing tennis. Without any particular thought or intervention you are able to hit the ball back over the net and feel good about it at the same time. It could be when you are meeting someone new or being served a meal. These processes are happening right now as you read this text. Whether you choose to or not, and whether you are aware of it or not, you are in the middle of an entrancing creative interaction that is, moment by moment, changing your life. From your experience in this moment you are preparing yourself for your next experience. This is achieved through the process of taking what you have learnt and applying this to your next moment to create a better experience. This is happening inside you and around you, to some degree, a dozen times each second. We are only consciously aware of the bigger and slower events, but even these are processed faster than we think. How often have you played a game of tennis and the more you *tried* to win the worse you played?

So, how do we step out of the winner/loser world, like Neo in *The Matrix,* and enter a creative world? It is a very different place of mind and heart. Instead of being in a world that pulls things apart into winners and losers, in the creative world you are connected and engaged. To understand this we need to look at the differences between the way we respond in the winner/loser world and the way we respond in the creative world. You can then understand and be aware of which world you are in. Shortly I will introduce the *8 Differences* between the winner/loser world and the creative world. These begin the process of defining the two worlds, but before we examine the 8 Differences, I just want to clarify what stress does to us from the biological view. It is important at this point for you to be absolutely clear what prolonged stress is doing to us and why I believe that the winner/loser world can no longer be tolerated.

♦♦♦ WHY BOTHER CHANGING? ♦♦♦
WE'VE DONE OKAY SO FAR, HAVEN'T WE?

Bliss will not be found by pretending that the winner/loser world does not exist or does not concern you – of course it does. When you career down the rapids of a river you cannot pretend that the rocks are not there. All that will happen is that your lack of acceptance will get you hurt. It is necessary to stare the winner/loser world in the face and live with it, but not be ruled by it; to be able to live in it, but know that you are not of it.

Richard Hill

People might well say we have done okay so far. I don't know how, but this is probably because the winner/loser world allows us to have opinions based only on our isolated experience. We know that things are not getting better - they are getting worse. Things may seem to be alright for some. The point is, however, that we have not been alright for quite some time and we have become used to it. The stress and 'craziness' we are noticing today is not new, it just can't be ignored any more. Perhaps there is a similarity in the way we have dealt with global warming. The first cautions were given in the mid 1950s, but now our melting polar icecaps, climate changes and increased species extinction is just too much to ignore. We need to recognise the winner/loser world and the damage it is doing to the human race.

Surprisingly, it is important to remember that stress is a natural process and is very healthy in the right conditions. It is the prolonged state of stress that damages you. We are designed to cope with *acute* stress. Before modern civilisation, acute stress may have been cause by physical challenges like chasing down another animal for food or running away from a predator. When stress becomes *chronic* we are soon in deep trouble. Below is a comparison in relation to various body parts and systems.

Acute Stress	Chronic Stress
Brain	
* increased alertness	* impaired memory
* reduced pain perception	* higher risk of depression
* reduced emotional reaction	* limitation on new learning
* limited planning and rationalisation	* reduction of empathy
Thymus Gland Immune Tissues	
* immune system readies for injury	* immune system deteriorates
	* increased illness
	* reduced wellness
Circulatory System	
* heart beats faster	* increased blood pressure
* blood vessels constrict to bring more blood	* increased cortisol in blood
	* disturbance of insulin balance
Adrenal Glands	
* secretion of hormones to mobilize energy supplies	* these hormones act to slow the recovery from stress
Reproductive Organs	
* reproductive functions are temporarily suppressed	* higher risk of infertility and miscarriage

In addition to the problems for the reproductive system, it has been found that the stressful nature of the workplace increases the amount of testosterone in women which not only affects their sexual fertility, but also their sexuality and aggressiveness. Men are also affected by these changes.

Prolonged stress is not something that you can put up with. Quite the opposite. We are no more capable of living a life under persistent stress than is an elephant capable of climbing Mount Everest. This is a clear and pressing reason why the winner/loser world is not only driving us crazy, but also doing us a lot of damage. Our heads are full of crazy beliefs that push us to accept behaviour that is downright dangerous. We may believe we are 'soldiering on', but we are not designed to ignore our warning mechanisms. Stress is literally killing some of us through premature illness and suicide. For others it is symbolically killing us with the depressing effect of persistent unhappiness and lack of fulfilment. We don't need to do either.

This information is not meant to scare, although it certainly made *me* stop and think. I hope it has done that for you too. Now, let's get right down to it and find out how to *do* something about all this. The 8 Differences will begin a practical understanding of the two worlds and lead us into the shift that comes from taking the 'red pill'.

✦✦✦ 8 DIFFERENCES ✦✦✦

*When a person falls over it is not just about helping them up,
we must be mindful of what we are helping them up into.
People might be falling over as an intuitive escape from a place
that is doing them harm. To help them up just to return them
to that place seems almost cruel*

Richard Hill

There are probably countless differences between the 'winner/loser world' and the 'creative world', but I have selected 8 pairs of words that give a good overall picture. These are a basic set of clear and distinct differences between the winner/loser world and the creative world. If you find yourself approaching your experiences in the ways of the left hand list, then it is reasonable to say that you are operating in a winner/loser way. If, however, you find that you approach your experiences in the ways of the right hand list, then you are operating in a creative way. I hope that many readers find that they already operate in the creative way at various times. I feel safe to predict that when you *did* operate in a creative way you felt better, enjoyed yourself more and felt closer to the other people involved.

This is the first step in the program: in your day-to-day experience observe the way you behave. If you feel stressed or worried or disconnected from others, then look to see if what you are doing and the way you are thinking is based on the winner/loser world ways. The process is to replace the winner/loser world approach with the creative world's different approach. You will most likely feel a huge emotional weight lift from your shoulders (particularly when you remove the fear of losing) and a sense of fascination rise as you open your mind to the additional possibilities you can create.

First, I will simply list the words in opposing columns, and then follow that with a more detailed explanation.

WINNER/LOSER WORLD	CREATIVE WORLD
1. EXCLUSION	INCLUSION
2. EVENTS	LESSONS/OPPORTUNITIES
3. INSTRUCTION	INFORMATION
4. COMPETITION	INSPIRATION
5. RESULT	OUTCOME
6. PROBABILITY	POSSIBILITY
7. TRANSACTION	INTERACTION
8. ARROGANCE	CONFIDENCE

1. EXCLUSION/ INCLUSION

EXCLUSION (winner/loser world)
The winner/loser world prefers and encourages isolated, separate or disconnected endeavour, and so there is a greater tendency to exclude. To exclude is to block things out, shut things out, push things out and not let things in. Exclusion results in a restriction of what is allowed into your environment. That doesn't mean that other people aren't involved in your experience, but they are excluded from the final act of winning. The winner is rewarded and so there is more to gain by not sharing. Rewards and benefits are both an attraction and a temptation in the winner/loser world.

Exclusion can also be used to make someone feel like a loser: "Let me do that. You're doing it wrong." It can show that you are individually strong and capable: "No thanks. I don't need any help." Exclusion is largely about focussing power. Those being excluded have no power and those doing the exclusion have a lot. Winners usually control the power, but power by exclusion has the price of limiting possibilities and opportunities.

Imagine an artist's palette. It is harder for a painter to create interesting colours when there are only a few tints to work with. How much more frustrating is it when other colours are available, but you are not allowed to use them? Exclusion happens in the workplace when information is limited. It happens at school when someone is excluded from a social group or they are victimised by a bully. It happens at home when there is an overt display of favouritism toward someone. It happens when you are not earning enough money to afford certain things. We even do it to ourselves when we believe that we are not good enough to be involved in something. You might believe you are not pretty enough to go to the party. You might believe you are not clever enough to apply for the job. You might believe you are not good enough to be loved. Exclusion can come from many directions and it is *always* unpleasant.

INCLUSION (creative world)
In order to maximise the creative process it is not only preferred, but essential for you to include as many elements as possible. Inclusion is about acceptance, although acceptance is not about blind agreement or being submissive. Acceptance is about acknowledgement, recognition and respect, balanced with a healthy dose of caution and consideration.

Inclusion is more than just being tolerant. Tolerance is a benign form of exclusion that can make you *appear* to be inclusive (although it can be a creative stepping-stone toward inclusion). To include is to take things as they come and as they are, and allow them to be creative elements of your experience.

Imagine again the artist's palette. If you include all the colour tints possible then you are in a much better position to create the colours that express your vision. You have much better options and possibilities. Inclusion is also about overcoming the displeasure of exclusion. We can expend a lot of energy trying to be included, just to show that we are a winner. If you find yourself excluded in one direction, try turning around and looking for what is in a different direction. It may be a pleasant surprise. The importance of the creative world is not *where* you participate, but *that* you participate. You may even choose to include yourself in the experience of being excluded so that you can learn about the people and the situation. Learning and understanding will always enhance your creative possibilities.

2. EVENTS / LESSONS

EVENTS (winner/loser world)
The winner/loser world is based around events – what *has* happened and *will* happen. An experience is not an event until it has happened. An imagined event is almost as real because it has happened in the mind. From events we are able to determine who is the winner and who is the loser, be it past or future. In the present moment there is no readily definable winner or loser.

During a race the competitors display a range of shifting fortunes. One is in the lead, and then another seems to make up ground. The leader begins to tire and the back-runner skirts the field on the outside. All of these descriptions are focussed on what is happening in the race in relation to who will win. This objective view is very different from the runners. They have a subjective experience where they are doing their best to run the race. Each step leads to the next and the runner is continuously changing and modifying their action in order to maximise their performance. No one knows who is going to win until they reach the finish line.

In life there is no finish line (perhaps not even at death). Even though it helps to break down the marathon of life into sections that doesn't mean that we have stopped participating in the present experience. The race continues whether you are paying attention or not. Life is the present moment. Events are not. As John Lennon said, "Life is what happens to you while you are making other plans."

We also imagine into the future. Because of this we have developed an interesting aspect of human behaviour: we tend not to attempt something that we don't believe we have a reasonable chance of achieving. This attitude is designed for life-and-death situations where a risky decision could cost your life. In the winner/loser world this instinct is unnaturally applied to non life-threatening situations. Mostly these are just socially threatening situations. Why study for exams when you don't believe you will pass? Why go for the better job if you don't believe you can get it? Why do anything where you might end up being a loser? It is easier and, arguably, more successful, to stick to what you have done well in the past in order to maintain a winning positioning in the present: "You just remember what I've done for you." "This is the way I've always done it and this is the way I'm doing it now."

It is, of course, impossible to escape a past event, because the past cannot be changed or altered (allowing for psychological delusion and issues of memory). We talk so often of 'moving on' from an event as if it is *possible* to remain in the past. We 'move on' from an event by the simple nature of time. It is only what we have *learnt* that can travel with us after an event. We are simply unable to be in the past. It is the negative feelings *about* the event that we carry in the present. Guilt in the present is hung on past events: "If only I hadn't done that." Fear of repeating past failures cause a host of problems: "I'll never be able to forgive myself." "I've been hurt before." "I can't go through that again." The present can almost cease to exist under the pressure of today's guilt about yesterday's event.

Case example: Mary and Ron were arguing all the time. Ron was careful with money, but Mary found that he made it impossible to buy the kids what they needed. She had given up on ever having an interesting social life. Whenever an argument flared up Ron would remind Mary of the time that she sent their credit card into a debt that took a year to repay. She would counter with the time that their daughter couldn't go on the school camp because they hadn't paid in time and how she cried for days eventually getting sick and missing a week of school.

Who was more right and more justified in winning the argument? No one. Mary defended herself as having learnt from the experience and Ron defended himself as being very sorry, but neither were interested in what was learnt. The past events were used as weapons to get the upper hand and win the argument. For as long as they prefer to be winners instead of lovers, they exclude themselves from happiness.

LESSONS/OPPORTUNITIES (creative world)

Every event is an opportunity to learn and grow. An event is just an experience. Every experience is filled with thousands of tiny events that show us what is working and what is not and allows us to sense what feels good and what doesn't. Events allow us to test ourselves and discover what lies within us and what lies within others. It also shows us about the environment we live in. Because we cannot travel back in time, an event ceases to be an element of our current experience. It is not something that can contribute to the creative process of *this* moment. Yesterday's experience is benign in the present. What we have *learnt* from the experience, however, travels with us through time. So, the lessons we learnt in the past become opportunities to create better and more satisfying experiences in the present and the future.

When others are living in a past event it can be very difficult for you in the present. The truth remains, however, that any difficulty you are experiencing is what you are experiencing *now*. From this you can learn. You can learn to understand the other people's difficulties and maybe help with their process of leaving the past in the past. It is what you create from what is available that marks the strength of the creative world.

Events leave us stuck and rigid and there is little happiness in that. Lessons enhance our opportunities. You can't cry over spilt milk, but you can clean up the mess, perhaps invent a better milk carrier. You might think about what allowed you to be so clumsy. It might be no more than a one-off unfortunate action. Someone once told me that a good cook is not someone who can bake a cake, but someone who can create something useful with a burnt one.

3. INSTRUCTION / INFORMATION

INSTRUCTION (winner/loser world**)**
Instruction is to be *told* what to do. Instruction is specific and detailed and is given so that it will be followed. Instructions, quite reasonably, are based on previous successful results and practices. This will maximise the chance of future success (as long as the same result is all that is wanted). Instruction, however, can make you feel as though you are not as clever as the person giving you the instruction (which may be true). It can also reinforce the idea that the person giving the instructions is more important and, therefore, more of a winner than the person being instructed. This tends to motivate people to disobey instructions in order to prove their independence and feel like winners again. Being instructed can isolate you from personal development and experience because it redirects your focus to compliance or rebellion.

It is interesting to note that compliance and rebellion are often just two sides of the same coin. Both acknowledge that the instructions and the instructor are a threat and a dominating influence. Instruction does not need to have such a negative effect, but it does in the winner/loser world. In the creative world the purpose of instruction is very different. In fact, it is not *instruction* at all. The winner/loser world gives importance to the person who believes they are in a dominant position. 'Knowledge is power' may be true in the winner/loser world. Because of this attitude an instructor can behave in a very condescending manner, which only goes to make you feel like a loser. They are using their knowledge to elevate their importance or diminish someone else's.

Instruction given in a winner/loser world way can actually cause the trainee to be less knowledgeable. You can feel so dominated by the rules that you stop using your initiative. The true power of knowledge is not *having* it, but what you *create* with it. Having a million facts in your head does not necessarily give you wisdom or even plain 'common sense'.

Case example: John was working on a building site as a casual labourer. The boss was a very difficult person who wanted everything done a particular way, and it was starting to drive John crazy. The boss told him how to carry, how to shovel dirt, how to do every task, however simple. On the first day of John's second week he was asked to sand the old paint off several second-hand doors. John was told exactly how to move the electric sander over the door and that he should start in the corner and move methodically across the grain of the wood. John listened patiently, but felt himself boiling inside. The boss left him to it. After a few minutes the boss came back and to John's amazement, immediately scolded John for not starting in the *other* corner of the door. The boss was completely surprised and couldn't understand it when John threw the sander at him and stormed off the job. John was not going to be treated like an idiot any more and the only way to win was to quit. What a waste.

INFORMATION (creative world)
Information is material that *informs* us. When we are informed we are aware. The purpose of instruction is to share information. Some information is obvious and we are readily aware of what it means and how we can implement it.

Sometimes it is not so obvious and it may be necessary to follow instructions 'parrot fashion' as we gradually understand how to use the information. Information is just like adding more colours to the artist's palette. These colours require testing and experiment to fully appreciate their value.

Creative world instruction is the *giving* of a piece of information. It can be said that the only difference between a teacher and a pupil is a little information. In the creative world information is even more than that. Information increases your opportunities and your possibilities by providing more 'stuff' to create with. The best creative response to an instruction may well be to follow it to the letter. Cooking is a good example. Following the recipe is the best way to learn what the author of the recipe is doing. Experimenting with the instructions depends on a number of factors. Sticking to the recipe is a great idea if you are not a good cook. This is neither compliance nor rebellion, just a good use of information.

From information we create. This means that everything outside us is information. No information can affect you negatively. How you respond to or process that information can have some effect, but this is not the information itself. Whatever happens to you or is said to you or you become aware of is information that will be included in the creative process of your experience. Someone may tell you that you are stupid, but instead of it being a hurtful insult or criticism, it is, in itself, interesting information. There is a lot of information within that comment that warrants further investigation. Information can trigger dozens of questions, which is, of course, the need for more information. Why do they think I'm stupid? What is happening that motivates them to say that to me? Why do they not care if I get upset? Am I really stupid or is this some emotional issue of theirs? Maybe they need some help and this is a clumsy way of getting my attention? There is a lot to learn here. Getting upset and defensive puts you in winner/loser mode and simply closes off any opportunity to learn and create a better outcome. In the creative world it is possible for everything that happens to be interesting information, not an emotional disturbance.

4. COMPETITION / INSPIRATION

COMPETITION (winner/loser world**)**
Competition is the process that produces winners. The battle is to find who is better, what is better, who is first and what the winning strategy is. Competition will focus your energy toward a winning goal. This could be a job or a promotion. It could be coming first in the class at school or achieving the highest mark in exams. It could be about managing your retirement better. It can be all sorts of things, but they are all about being better or achieving more than anyone else. 'Winners are grinners'. This is largely because winners are rewarded and losers are not. Winners are usually a very small group, often just one. That means that when a competition is completed most of the participants are losers. During his presentation of the best actor award at the Academy Awards, Paul Hogan sardonically announced, "The winners smile and the losers have to". It was a delightfully cheeky description of how the losers have to try and look as though they haven't lost and all is well, but everyone knows that they are disappointed.

Competition, in the winner/loser world motivates you to try harder and do better because being the best makes you better in everyone's eyes – whether you actually feel like that or not. Prestige is a great reward, let alone things like money and popularity. The winner/loser world keeps throwing up more and more irresistible rewards and temptations for winning. At some point these rewards can outweigh our better judgement. Winning at all costs because there is so much at stake has caused great shame, heartache and pain. Equally, there are often more and more unacceptable consequences of being a loser.

I don't believe that winning is a bad thing. I do believe, however, that it can get destructive when it is the *dominating* goal.

The suicide statistics alone show that losing in the winner/loser world has devastating consequences. Competition is evident in so many things. The clothes you wear show if you are a winner or a loser in the fashion stakes. Fashion is a hugely competitive part of our daily life. Being too fat or too thin or too tall or too short has devastated the emotions and the health of many people. 'Keeping up with the Jones' is an expression that has been around for a long time and symbolises the suburban competition to be as good as your neighbour: the bigger house, the bigger car, the brighter children and so much more all to establish who is the winner, who is the best.

Many children give up any thoughts of being a winner quite early in life. Because they are measured only in the competitive systems of the winner/loser world they soon learn who are the natural winners. The constant pressure to win permeates our thinking processes until we don't even realise we are making decisions and taking actions based on our chances of winning, rather the opportunity of experiencing. People only do what they know they can win. Some people make losing their winning thing. "My life is so awful. Nothing goes right for me!" In the winner/loser world you can make some success in being the worst at something. Bizarre isn't it. The competitive edge often makes it all the way into the bedroom.

Case Example: Jason is very successful in his work. So is his wife, Wendy. Socialising with these two is a real ordeal. A simple picnic in the park is like a mini Olympic Games. Everything they do is like an event and their friends have to praise the winner. Although they compete on the stereotypical basis that males are stronger and females are more sensitive and creative, they often take the game into each other's court. Wendy has challenged Jason to an arm wrestle more than once. She has even won a couple of times. Jason took up cooking just to show that he could do better. Their relationship is energetic, vigorous and volatile. What they find hard to understand now is why their love life has gone. It has always been great, but now there doesn't seem to be any connection. However, it is not hard to see that when two people stand on opposite sides of the ring and only relate to each other when the fight is on, they will, one day, find that they become bored with the competition - in this case, with each other. No relationship can survive when the participants act like they are on different teams. If you stand apart and only seek to conquer, you eventually get tired of winning *or* losing and there is no desire to play any more. Jason and Wendy are just finding that out.

INSPIRATION (creative world**)**
Inspiration comfortably absorbs the concept of winning. Winning, of course, is just one piece of information about an experience. The motivation to excel yourself in the creative world is the exhilaration of creating an experience that you have never had before - that no one has had before. The truth is that whatever is happening to you at this moment has never happened to you before. It may be similar to what you have done before, but it is never exactly like before.

Life is a process of continuous experiences that take you somewhere you have never been before. This may be to a position called winning, but it also may not. Regardless, you have never been in this moment before and you are not the same as you have ever been before. There is a host of interesting information of which you are not yet aware. You have never done what you are about to do. There are changes in you. They may be subtle and perhaps imperceptible to your conscious awareness, but thankfully the creative process is not limited to what we think we know. The next time you give your partner a hug it will be different to any hug you have ever given. To not give the hug because you gave one earlier is to have slipped back into the winner/loser world. The presence of your partner, the love you have for them, the physical desires of human beings and a host of other things are, through the creative process, inspiring you to connect, hug and change the world again, because you have never had that hug before.

Romance is just one example in an inspiring playground of life that is new every day. So is your work, your play, your friendships, your schoolwork, your morning cup of tea with a friend, your quiet moments alone and every other experience you have. Life is just so inspiring when you don't *have* to win. If you are the fastest swimmer in the world, then be the fastest. If not, then be the fastest you can be. Certainly it would be nice to have all the winner/loser world accolades and all the endorsement dollars, but you can only be the fastest you can be. The surprising thing is that when you strive through inspiration you can achieve much more because you are not limited to just winning.

Inspiration can take you places that you never even thought you might go whereas competition only takes you to the finish line.

5. RESULT / OUTCOME

RESULT (winner/loser world**)**
In the winner/loser world goals are set in order to pre-determine what will be a winning result. When a goal is reached then the process is complete. New goals are required and are often prompted by competition. Good results are a successful conclusion to a process. Bad results are a failure to achieve the goal.

If you have achieved a good result then the rewards can be taken and you can move on to the next goal. If it is a bad result then you have to start again. Perhaps you need to retrace your steps or even ditch the whole idea and find a different direction. You have to examine what went wrong, who made mistakes, where the failures occurred and if there is anything that can be salvaged from the disaster. Bad results are a huge loss. This all sounds very negative, but that is the winner/loser world way.

So, how do we know the difference between something that deserves our persistence and something that is simply not possible and should be abandoned? In the winner/loser world the only way to gauge that is by the measure of winning or losing. If your goal is to make a lot of money then you must persist until you do. There may be some very interesting things that occur along the way, but lots of money is definitely a 'winning thing' so *that* remains the focus.

The difficulty with results is that they are based on the foundation of goals that were set in the past. Goals are guesstimates of what will be a good result in the future. Future prediction is always clouded with a degree of uncertainty. When this uncertainty is ignored you end up with the rigidity of being forced to achieve a goal that may well be no longer valid or relevant. We see this in the 'generation gap' where the goals that parents set for their children may not be the best or even relevant any more. Times change and rigid expectations have caused a great deal of heartache and disappointment even when people are doing their best. Unfortunately the winner/loser world has very little flexibility.

OUTCOME (creative world)

An outcome is a step in a continuous process. In the creative world the pathway of life does not stop. It may shift, alter, have gaps, pauses and diversions, but there is no possibility of going back and doing it again. You can do it anew, but never again. The pathway of life only has the opportunity to move to the next step. Our experiences come from our interaction with the world us. These interactions create an outcome. Each outcome is a step along the path. Importantly, each outcome quickly becomes a part of our past experience and learning. This adds more to us and alters the world around us. This creates a 'new' you and a 'new' world in which you will interact. Life is made up of this ongoing interactive process. An outcome is just another step to another outcome. An outcome is part of the ongoing process that constructs our experience.

In the creative world there is no opportunity to lose because failure is just a momentary outcome that leads to another step. An outcome that takes you in a direction you don't wish to go is an *undesirable* outcome. The response to an undesirable outcome is to look for what can be learnt, and seek to improve the next interaction, the next step. If an outcome is *desirable,* then it is reasonable and preferable to continue in that direction.

So, how do you know if an outcome is desirable or undesirable? This is a bit complicated, but that is discussed more in Section 2. Put simply, how you think and also how you *feel* will be a clear message. The difficulty is that your feelings may be responding to whether you believe you are winning or losing so you need to separate those first. Having done that (I explain this more in the 6 Practices) you will know by your feelings of happiness or contentment, your degree of frustration, whether you feel energetic and inspired or disappointed and forlorn. You will know the difference between the stress of banging your head against a winner/loser wall or the stress of motivation that will inspire you to find that something extra or to be confident to take a different direction.

A result binds you or sends you backwards. An outcome takes you somewhere.

6. PROBABILITY / POSSIBILITY

PROBABILITY (winner/loser world)
Probability is the *likelihood* that something is achievable. Human beings have a natural inclination to do what is probable and to avoid it or give up if it is not (although we can also persist in 'flogging a dead horse', but that is another issue). In the winner/loser world there is pressure to achieve a winning result. Probability is restricted when expectation and anticipation is limited to winning. We will avoid things where we fear failure. When success and failure are defined by something as limiting

as the winner/loser world, then we are constricted even further by these predetermined results.

Students sitting for their end-of-school exams can buckle under the pressure of having to achieve a particular score. They have a set goal. The greater the pressure the more difficult it is for the student to perform their best. Competition increases the fear of failure and the body instincts respond as if failure is a life and death issue. We have not yet evolved a body that understands the difference between real threat and imagined threat. This is why stress and anxiety become so debilitating. Probability may protect us from attempting things where we might lose our life, but it debilitates our sense of adventure and discovery. We limit ourselves to what is probable on a day-to-day basis.

Low self-esteem compounds the effect of what we believe is probable. As more and more seems to be improbable there is a greater feeling of not being able to do anything, which only goes to dampen self-esteem more. You may not believe you are pretty enough to go to the dance, and this is compounded by an estimation that it is not probable you will be able to dance with the person you are keen on. On top of that you are scared by the thought of having to compete because you don't believe you will win, and so you stay home. All the other *possible* outcomes that might occur are now removed from your experience.

It is these other possible outcomes that we lose in the winner/loser world.

Case example: Simon was an apprentice bricklayer. He spent one week a month at the local TAFE college studying theory and specialised techniques. He was great at working with his hands, but had very little confidence in his brain. High school was not a good experience for him. He enjoyed TAFE and the practical work, but the maths really troubled him. He tried hard, but was only able to scrape through. He had to pass maths in order to get his qualification and the upcoming exam was four weeks away. He was so stressed he was making mistakes in his practical work as well. It seemed to him that it couldn't work. He might as well quit and just be a labourer. The money was better anyway.

After a lot of coaxing Simon went to his teacher and talked about it. The teacher immediately volunteered to help him. Simon was totally surprised. He didn't think that teachers would do that. Twice a week Simon would meet with the teacher. When the exam came Simon was still quite scared, but he felt he had a chance. His final result was not great, but it was a pass. He was on his way to his tradesman's ticket.

Simon thought he had no chance of passing maths and almost believed that it was a good idea to take the path with a higher probability of success. This meant going back to labouring. It meant lower pay, worse conditions and never learning a trade, but at least he wouldn't fail. It is obviously easier to succeed in something that is easy to do, but there is little to learn from what you already know.

POSSIBILITY (creative world)
Possibility is an open-ended concept. Possibility includes outcomes that we may not have imagined. If you try something without the constraint of probability, then you allow for the possibility of an unexpected outcome. This is a problem in the winner/loser world where progress is charted along a path of predetermined results, but in the creative world those restrictions don't apply.

This is not to say that we can do everything and anything. The creative world is not an excuse to be irresponsible or negligent. Quite the opposite. If you allow the creative process to work with all that is available you will tend to act in a direction that is beneficial (see Harmony, Section 2). More important, however, is that in the creative world an outcome is not a final result. If an outcome is one of the possibilities that you don't want, then you simply continue the process. In fact, the process will continue anyway. The process continues because the door is open to possibilities in the creative world.

Possibility means that *all* the things that are in your capacity and your environment can be utilised, investigated and tested. When the doors of possibility are open you can even discover things about yourself that you didn't know. Probability is limited to what we know from our past experience. There are many qualities, talents and capabilities that only rise to the surface when an experience prompts a need. If all we do is what we know we can do, then we may never discover what we don't know we can do.

The poet, Thomas Grey, wrote in his *Elegy to a Country Churchyard* of the unexpressed possibilities of the farmers buried in the churchyard. They might have been politicians or great writers, "Some mute inglorious Milton here may rest". The adventures of our experience give us the opportunity to release our potential and discover our unpredictable contributions.

When my daughter was sitting for her high school finals I was asked in a radio interview what my expectations were. I answered that I had none. The interviewer was shocked. I went on to explain that I wanted her to do well in her exam, but that whatever result she achieved we would create something out of it. "In our household," I explained, "We have no expectations, but all possibilities are entertained." Rather than competing to win she was free to discover what she was able to achieve. The exam became a mechanism that she could use to appreciate how she was performing compared to others. This is very different from doing an exam to find out what the system considers to be your value. I believe this gives greater scope for an enjoyable life.

In essence, possibilities are an endless source of opportunity whereas probabilities restrict us to specific opportunities.

7. TRANSACTION / INTERACTION

TRANSACTION (winner/loser world**)**
Transaction is a negotiation where the desired result is to get
what you want while giving away as little as possible. In a
transaction there is reservation and constraint. When you are
conducting a transaction it is wise to hold your cards to your
chest. Bargaining for a price is a good example of a common
transaction where the seller demands a high price and the buyer
offers a low price. The winner is the person who gets the best
price. The more you can 'stiff the other guy' the more successful
you have been.

Most transactions may be less competitive than that, but they
are still based on a 'you scratch my back and I'll scratch yours'
approach. It would be silly to lay all your cards on the table in a
transaction. To reveal everything puts you at a disadvantage,
especially if the other person is not telling the truth about what
they are revealing. In business there is perhaps some
justification for this. The business world is largely an invention
of the winner/loser world. Still, I would rather it weren't like
that.

Unhappiness and stress arise when transactions take place in
emotional matters. Relationships often suffer from this. One
partner holds back an emotion until the other one treats them in
a certain way or they do it as a punishment because they have
acted in a certain way, "I am not going to be happy with you
after what you just did." Emotional transaction can be very
damaging to children, eg. "You can't have a hug until you've
been good." Transaction is the give and take of the
winner/loser world and winning is decided by who gets the
most while giving the least.

Watching a child trying to negotiate with their parent for
permission to do something is often like watching a wily poker
player. Each time the parent says no, they up the ante and reveal

a little more. You know that your child is learning the winner/loser world way when they are able to play a resounding trump card to get what they want.

Anger is often used as a transaction. Each card that is played reveals a more dangerous volcano of threat. Demure and seductive games can be played in the same way. If the only goal of the game is to win then the players are all at risk. Parents will often say no and continue to do so even if the child provides a good argument. Winning will override good sense or, at least, reasonable request. Transaction is a fool's game, but the winner/loser world makes it the only alternative.

Case example: Betty's four-year-old girl, Marsha, was being very difficult. Betty was concerned, but she was more concerned with the sorts of things she was saying. Marsha would be very mean and say hurtful things like, "I hate you, mummy. I wouldn't care if the vacuum cleaner sucked you up and you were dead." Marsha would sometimes sit patting the cat and completely ignoring Betty's instructions. Once she threw her fork at Betty and caused an injury that drew blood. It seemed that Marsha was too young to have thought of these things herself. The session turned to a discussion about Betty and other members of the family. We discovered that the marriage was going through a difficult time. Betty suspected that her husband was having an affair. He was always late home and often had to go away on business trips. Betty was shocked to realise how she was emotionally blackmailing her husband both as a punishment and to try and get him to tell her the truth. She could remember saying things like, "You're never here. You might as well be dead." "You're not getting a hug from me. I'm far too busy." She would often not say anything to him when he got home and just keep on doing whatever she was doing. The issue of Betty's marriage is a different story, but clearly Marsha had learnt how to say cruel things in a household of emotional transaction.

INTERACTION (creative world)
Interaction is the uninhibited coming together of all the elements involved. By allowing everything to mix freely these elements are able to respond and react with each other to create an outcome. Interaction is about openness and unconditional positive regard. This is a delightful expression that is used in psychotherapy and it means what the words directly imply: by imposing no conditions or expectations and taking a positive outlook and attitude we create a safe environment that engenders respect. Interaction is about allowing the elements to interact freely on the assumption that the outcome will be beneficial and helpful when winning is no longer the dominating goal. This is reasonable to expect in a mutually respectful situation.

This may sound risky because it could leave you open to an unpleasant experience. Not an unreasonable caution, but a bad experience is more likely to indicate that you have slipped back into the winner/loser world. In the creative world, where winning and losing are no concern, there is little danger. In my day-to-day activities I don't expect everyone to be open, connected and caring for my welfare, but because I have no fear of losing, I am more likely to interact even when I'm not sure of their intention. I know that if I want to create the best outcome I need to include as many elements as possible. Openness is worth the risk in the creative world because there is much less at risk if it doesn't work out.

Smiling at a stranger in the creative world doesn't mean that you keep smiling until they smile back. It doesn't mean that you get annoyed if they react unkindly. The process of unconditional positive regard is where you are open to others and respectfully accepting of how they are open to you.

It's really about being honest and straightforward. We hold back what we fear can be used against us to damage our position as a winner or make us a loser. In the winner/loser world this is a reasonable fear. When dealing with winner/loser world people or situations it is sensible to be mindful of this. If you find that you have to transact instead of interact then it is just a matter of knowing this and not allowing yourself to fall back into the harmful grasp of living the winner/loser world way.

8. ARROGANCE / CONFIDENCE

ARROGANCE (winner/loser world**)**
Arrogance means that I believe I am better than you. In the winner/loser world you can 'psyche out' an opponent just by your arrogance. If they begin to think that their probability of success is lower they are more likely to give up. You might call it self-confidence, but when it is used to maximise the chances of winning then I think it moves beyond a sense of personal strength and becomes a weapon to give an advantage. An arrogant belief in your capabilities is used to boost the ego and intimidate those around you in order to win.

Bullying is a harsh example of arrogance. In this case the arrogance is often an expression of low self-esteem and a belief that if they don't get you first then you will get them. This, of course, doesn't seem to make sense when bullies pick on the smaller or less fortunate, but the reason is often to impress their peer group rather than actually hurt the victim. If the peer group keeps the bully on a pedestal then the goal has been achieved.

Wealthy people are often seen as arrogant, although this must considered in relation to the jealousy of people with less money. When a rich person carries on as if they have some special privilege just because of their money it may be because they believe it is true. In the winner/loser world it very often is true. It is not uncommon for lottery winners to behave with this arrogance even though they have done little to earn the money and the right to privilege.

Arrogance will continue to be a difficulty where winning and being treated like a winner is a socially acceptable practice. But that is what the winner/loser world creates and what the winner/loser world problem engenders.

CONFIDENCE (creative world)
Confidence comes when you are able to express what you believe to be your strengths and talents. There is strong support for the idea that we have an intuitive sense of what it is possible for us to be. When we are able to express this potential in our external experience there is a sense of satisfaction and stability. Some describe this as a state of harmony, which I describe at greater length in Section 2.

Confidence is also founded on the feeling that you are not alone and that you are supported with unconditional positive regard. Your support may only come from a handful of people, but that is enough. Confidence is an expression of personal stability. It is also an expression of having no fear of consequences. This is almost impossible in the winner/loser world because it is so easy to be toppled from the winner's pedestal. In the creative world consequences are far less evident. The creative world, however, is not a fanciful world where everyone is perfect. It is a natural world and one of the lessons of the natural world is consequence. Consequence helps to reinforce the learning process, but not as a punishments like in the winner/loser world. Consequences can also be beneficial and positive.

Confidence to try something is truly a quality of the creative world. The principal restraint is fear of failure, but there is no failure in the creative world. It's just an undesirable outcome. I can remember when I was about 12 in my last day at Primary School and we were all being extremely 'naughty' and playing games. We started a game of spin-the-bottle. There must have been 30 kids. I don't think there were too many 'couples' at that age, so it was just adventurous fun. The bottle spun to me and I had to wait to see who I would kiss. The bottle landed on a girl whose name was Frances, I think. She wasn't one of the 'pretty' girls. I guess you would call her a 'geek' nowadays. Everybody assumed that I would not want to kiss her. The boys grabbed me and the girls grabbed Frances to make sure that I endured this horrible thing.

But I didn't think it was so terrible. We were playing a game and I was having my turn. I think back sometimes to the unintentional cruelty of the other kids. She was a nice enough girl, but everyone made her feel like a gorgon. I never saw her again after that day so I don't know whether she realised that I was quite happy to kiss her or whether she was overpowered by the taunting of the other children.

This story rose in my mind because I can remember my confidence in being able to kiss the 'ugly' girl without having to be forced. At 12 years old, what is 'good looking' anyway? Did she think I was arrogant as I pushed my mates away and willingly gave the kiss? These are the events of our lives that sit up like tags and remind us how we learnt things. We need to think about our lives. Epicurus would ask us to 'consider'.

◆◆◆◆◆◆◆◆◆◆◆

In order to find a balance between our inner and outer experience we need to make sense of life. These 8 Differences may go a long way to helping you make sense of what you have learnt from your life. Consider events that still bother you and see whether the 8 Differences shed a new light. If you can recognise that the principal problem was the imposition of the winner/loser world then you might like to re-consider what this means in light of the creative world. I am hoping that you feel more confident about yourself as you explore the process.

In the creative world, you feel like a strong individual, not because of *separation*, but because of *inclusion*. By simply allowing yourself to be a part of the world around you, the world around you becomes a part of you. Nothing works for you or against you - everything works *with* you. Even the difficult things that can disable you in the winner/loser world lose their destructive power in the creative world and become an inspiration for something better. Every experience provides helpful and productive information that inspires you. Each outcome becomes a stepping-stone in the continuous path of life experience. You are an integral part of a swirling galaxy of elements that is your environment, and there is no barrier to creative interaction. You are effortlessly engaged in a connected, sharing, communally expansive life. The future is full of possibilities. Escaping the winner/loser world occurs spontaneously when you cease to act as a separate and disconnected person. When you de-emotionalise the elements of winning and losing you can remove them as measures of your value as a human being. In the creative world, you are transported to a place where your drive is energised by inspiration and your emotional foundation is happiness.

So, how does the winner/loser world sneak up on us the way it does? Nobody *wants* to be depressed or stressed. The answer to that has come from my observation of clients and the issues that bothered them. I found that I could summarise almost every problem down to a set of 7 basic issues. The trick was that these issues didn't look like they were the problem. In fact they quite often looked like the way to solve their problem. I began to see these as tricksters with a very sneaky and devious nature. I call them the *7 Demons*. I wonder if they will be as much of a surprise to you as they were to me, but then that's how demons are.

♦♦♦ THE 7 DEMONS ♦♦♦

It's never just a game when you're winning.
George Carlin

This chapter is about how the winner/loser world gets under our skin and does so much emotional damage. I call this the 7 Demons because demons are things that get into us and cause division within us and around us. 'Demon' comes from the Greek *'daio'* meaning to divide or distribute.

In understanding the 7 Demons you will gain more insight into the winner/loser world and be able to better deal with the emotional difficulties it causes. Understanding the 7 Demons will also help you know which world you are in. These elements are demons when they make you feel bad and cause problems in your life. They are demons when they interfere and disrupt your enjoyment of life causing stress or emotional pain. Some of the demons do not exist in the creative world; others are completely changed in their effect.

I chose these particular 'demons' from my experience with clients at my clinic and my own life. Almost every problem that my clients experienced could be seen to be caused or affected by one or more of the 7 Demons. The reason why these demons are so difficult to resolve is that they are not just problems *within* the winner/loser world; they are *foundations* of its structure. They are part of the belief system that allows the winner/loser world to function. A belief system is very difficult to resolve. That is why these 'demons' are almost impossible to remove. It's like trying to get dry while you are still in the water.

It is important to add at this point, however, that there are a number of issues concerning mental health that are nothing to do with the winner/loser world or the creative world. There are conditions, states of mind and neurological complaints that require specialised treatment and care. I wish to make it clear that I am not advocating that understanding the creative world will cure such serious conditions. I am advocating, however, that the general level of depression that comes from the stress of trying to live in the winner/loser world can be radically improved. Also, conditions that develop because of the emotional distress caused by the winner/loser world can be avoided. It *may* also be true that severe conditions that are triggered by certain experiences might not be triggered in the creative world.

Again, I will start with a simple list, followed by deeper explanations. The bullet point 'thoughts' at the end of each explanation have come from things said by real people, collected here to aid your understanding.

7 DEMONS

1.	**RIGHT AND WRONG**
2.	**GOOD AND BAD**
3.	**EXPECTATION**
4.	**FAULT AND BLAME**
5.	**CRITICISM**
6.	**ISOLATION AND SEPARATION**
7.	**GUILT**

1. RIGHT AND WRONG

It's hard to think something so basic and seemingly virtuous could be a problem, but it *is* - in the winner/loser world. This demon, however, isn't the fundamental nature of right and wrong, but the power and prestige we gain in *being* right.

When you are right your opinion should be valued. Being right gives you the moral high ground and warrants respect. Being right means you should be obeyed. Sometimes you are right because of your opinions, ideas and actions, but it also might be your nationality, skin colour or social class. It can be your job or education. Whether it is personal or through your associations, it is definitely an advantage to be right.

Because it is an advantage, being right makes you a winner. This makes it something worth fighting for. In an argument the one who is right is the winner. The loser must be deemed as wrong. All too often, as I encounter in my clinic, couples argue and fight about who is right: "He/she is never wrong. I'm not allowed to have an opinion. It drives me crazy!" "I don't care what he/she is saying, it's not right."

I have seen friends stop talking to each other; families break apart; workplaces become unfriendly and unproductive; people of all ages become depressed and anxious; outbreaks of anger and violence both emotional and physical; and over nothing in particular, just the dogged determination to be right.

Think about the last few upsets or arguments you've had with someone. How many were, at the base of it, about who was right and who was wrong. Perhaps it was over whose opinion was to be followed, or about who was in charge. It may have been about trying to justify some action. It's often about who is the cleverest or the one who knows more or has done more. Too often it is about morals and values and who deserves respect and who doesn't. Mostly we argue about trivial things that are of no importance two days later, but the *fight* is about who is in control of the position of *being right*.

After it has been decided who is right then the other person, by default, is wrong. Logically, you follow who is right. Being right is rewarded with superiority, control and dominance. In the battle for right the ends can justify the means: threatening your partner; demoralising your children; saying hurtful things; being adamant and aggressively assertive.

Strange as it may seem, 'right and wrong' is one of the most damaging demons of the winner/loser world. These battles can readily spread from the bedroom, the playground or the workplace to much more serious places with much more serious weapons. This seemingly basic aspect of life - to know and live by what is right and wrong - can be manipulated into a battle that not only breaks hearts and minds, but kills.

In the winner/loser world, 'right and wrong' is the first and most destructive demon.

So, what is right and wrong?
There was a lovely film called 'K-pax' starring Kevin Spacey. He plays a man who claims to be from another planet called K-pax. He ends up in a psychiatric institution being cared for by a psychiatrist played by Jeff Bridges. Bridges listens to Spacey describe the society on K-pax where there were very few rules or controls. He asks how people on K-pax know what right from wrong. Spacey replied, "...every being in the universe knows right from wrong..."

This is an interesting idea. Do we really need to be told what is right from wrong? An essential description of rights and wrongs has risen independently across many cultures. The Ten Commandments are a good example. The essential elements are that you must not kill others or take possession of what is not yours. You must show respect to others and help them in their struggles as they should help you in yours. It may be safe to say that, broadly, we don't need any instruction on right and wrong, we know it on the inside.

Rules, regulations and the need to police them is really something else again. This is more about management than morals. In a large complex society like ours, knowing right from wrong doesn't mean that everyone will do it, so there is a need to impose some controls.

So, being right has a few more meanings than we might first think. In a system where rules take the responsibility for right and wrong out of the hands of the people there is a diminished need for reliance on personal morals and values. Living by the rules can become a virtue in itself. In rebellious circles not living by the rules is a virtue.

In the creative world it is easier to listen to your inner sense of right and wrong because it is not trying to win. In the creative world, it is about connecting your inner wellbeing with the wellbeing of the world around you. 'Right and wrong' is about respect for others and for yourself; connection and interaction; and positive regard for everything around you.

Here are some of the thoughts that cause emotional stress due to right and wrong.

- I'm in charge, so I am right.
- *You* can't be right because then *I* am wrong.
- The ideal is what is real; unless I reach the ideal I am a failure.
- There is only one way to reach a goal: the right way.
- No matter what I do, I am always wrong.
- I can never be wrong.
- If I am wrong, then what do I do next? I'm confused.
- Admitting you are wrong is a sign of weakness.
- Showing of any kind of emotion is wrong and a sign of weakness.
- Asking for help from someone else just shows you don't know what you're doing.

2. GOOD AND BAD

'Good' is a desired result and 'bad' is an undesired result. It's good when things work out the way you want. You can *feel* good. This usually means that you feel positive, uplifted and encouraged. It feels good to do things that make you feel good.

Feeling bad is the opposite. This usually means that you feel negative, disheartened and discouraged.

If we feel good when it works out the way we want, how do we *know* it's the way we want? We must have some expectation or predetermined goal. 'Good' becomes a demon because the winner/loser world demands that the result be a winner. So any result where you don't win is bad result. Any result that isn't like the one you planned is a bad result. Any result that doesn't meet your expectations is a bad result. That is a very restricted system. It is more likely that you will have a bad result because the parameters to win are so tight.

A bad result means that you are not a winner, which means you are a loser. If you are a loser you are all the bad things that that entails and all because you didn't get a good result. So a good result is worth fighting for. It might be worth cheating for. It might be worth doing a lot of things that you are not proud of or happy to do. You might need to spend more time away from your family. It might be stressful and leave you bad tempered. You might yell at the kids. There are a lot of things that we go through to be sure that we get a good result. In fact, we tolerate a lot of bad results to get a good result. The difference with those secondary bad results is that they weren't planned or expected so they don't seem to count in the winner/loser world. That is the way in which good and bad become demons.

In the creative world we don't have results we have outcomes. Each outcome teaches us something. One thing we may learn is that we didn't like the outcome, but that is different from the winner/loser world. In the winner/loser world the result is desired because of expectation. In the creative world the outcome may or may not be *desirable*, but this is just information that contributes to the next experience and the next outcome.

Case example: For every page that you are reading I have probably written 6 or 7 pages that weren't as desirable as this one. That's not to mention the notes and the hours of conversation with my ever-patient wife, Susie. But every page I wrote taught me something that contributed to the next page. I would probably like to keep altering and adding and subtracting words forever, but there has to be a moment when the writing stops and the printing begins.

Is this book a good result? For me, it is a very desirable outcome. It's not good *or* bad. In the creative world you are no longer dependent on results to feel good.

Here are some of the thoughts that cause emotional stress due to good and bad:

- I have no value in life unless I am successful.
- When do the troubles and problems cease? I'm tired of all this.
- I'll have to start again from scratch.
- What a waste of time.
- I went into this with the best of intentions. It just didn't do what I wanted.
- Nothing went to plan. It was a disaster.
- Don't try and tell me there's a positive in this mess. There's nothing.
- If we don't start getting some good results we're in big trouble.
- This relationship is nothing like I planned.
- I don't fit in here or anywhere else for that matter!

3. EXPECTATION

Expectations are the greatest burdens we carry on a day-to-day basis and very few of them make any sense when you genuinely stop and think about it. Most of our expectations are the things that we have to do to satisfy the requirements of winner/loser world which may have very little to do with our needs as a person. Things have to work out a certain way in order for us to be winners, to be successful, to be right and get a good result.

Expectation is synonymous with the word *should*. We *should* be this and we *should* be that and *should* do this and we *should* do it that way. We *need* things to work out the way they should because then everything will be okay. When everything is okay then we can relax, be happy and enjoy our lives. Trouble is that when things interact we don't have complete control over the outcome so we try to force a good result. As we saw earlier, a good result is very difficult to achieve and that difficulty is amplified by expectations. The more demanding and specific the expectations are, the fewer acceptable options we have.

Our hope that tomorrow will be a better day is severely limited if tomorrow is only a good day if it comes up to our expectations. This dilemma is the root of so much unhappiness. "Johnny's exam marks weren't what we expected. He's such a disappointment." "How could they have done that? I was doing everything right. Surely I can expect better treatment than that." "That's a lovely gift, but it's not really what I was expecting." "I'm doing the best that I can. What do they expect of me?"

Expectation kills possibility and completely shrouds the opportunity that an outcome presents. When someone is not good enough, who decided what *is* good enough? When we feel like a loser, who set the standard of being a winner? When you feel disappointed or a disappointment, what did you do wrong and why is it wrong? The message from these questions is that we don't question enough. We assume that the expectations of the winner/loser world are right and, so, that is exactly what we should do (there's that *should* word again). It sure is difficult to find out who you are, what you can do and what is your unique contribution when who you should be, what you should do and the contribution you should make is all predetermined. That is an impossible burden and a *very* sneaky demon.

Here are some of the thoughts that cause emotional stress due to expectation:

- If those in authority say this is the way it is supposed to be, then that is the way it is supposed to be.
- It is what you achieve rather than who you are that is important.
- If I have a failure or experience a set back in my efforts to change then I should give up.
- I am never successful in picking partners, so why try again!
- Stop the world; I want to get off.
- You've asked too much of me this time. I can't handle it.
- I can never accomplish the task facing me!
- Everybody is looking at me, just waiting for me to make a fool of myself!
- I am ugly and awful to look at!
- What is the sense of trying? I'll never get it right!
- Having kids has really changed things. I thought it would be different.

4. FAULT AND BLAME

When something goes wrong in the 'winner/loser world', it generally means that it 'hasn't gone the way it was supposed to', 'not the way it should', 'wasn't successful', 'didn't work' or 'failed'. The winner/loser world is principally based on the cause and effect system. There must be a reason if something fails and that reason will show where the fault is and what or who is to blame. Whoever or whatever is to blame is responsible for fixing it, sorting it out or working it out. Whatever it is, fault and blame is aimed at a loser and a loser deserves whatever they get.

If, by some misfortune, you end up in a losing situation it is much better not to be at fault. If it is at all possible you should shift the responsibility onto something or someone else. That shifts the failure elsewhere. This may sound unfair, but being to blame has consequences. No one invites punishment. Being 'at fault' automatically warrants punishment because you are wrong. Finding fault in others or deflecting blame from yourself is what the winner/loser world is all about.

Therapy for those who have had to accept blame is often about turning their negative feeling into a positive, finding the lessons, focussing on things that did work, realising that failure in one thing is not necessarily failure in everything and other very worthwhile ideas. These are all well and good, but when these things are done *in order* to help you manage in the winner/loser world there are problems. When therapy is just a way of turning losing into winning then you are still stuck in the winner/loser game. This is a fragile foundation that often founders later.

In the creative world there is no fault or blame game at all. If there have been errors of judgement, mistakes made, poor performance, or any of the winner/loser world faults, then they become valuable information that contribute to the next experience. There is no need to waste time with justification or blame shifting or any of the other disruptive winner/loser world practices. In the creative world you are always in the process of creating something more. Fault and blame shut down progress and the process. They are demons of distraction and disruption.

Here are some of the thoughts that cause emotional stress due to fault and blame:

- I don't attempt things I can't do well.
- There are so many roadblocks and pitfalls to keep me from succeeding. It is better just to give up and forget my goal.
- It's not my fault I am the way I am.
- I never asked to be born.
- Now that you have me, what are you going to do with me?

- I want you to fix me.
- How can I ever be happy, after how bad my life has been?
- My parents made me what I am today!
- I failed in the past; therefore, I am a failure today.
- Even if it is my fault, I can't afford to admit it.
- Just one mistake and every good thing I've done is forgotten.

5. CRITICISM

The Oxford dictionary says that criticism is not just finding fault, but making a statement or remark about it. Criticism raises a fault or failing into our awareness. We give it a voice. This applies to both public criticism and self-criticism (where we give it an inner voice – sometimes called the inner critic). As a demon, it even attacks things that appear to be winners and makes them losers. These attacks can be toward things we do, things we try, results we achieve and even our personality. Criticism publicly highlights shortcomings and failings to ensure a bad result.

Criticism makes you feel bad in a similar way to having a bad result. We all know how unpleasant criticism is and so it is often deliberately used to make us feel bad. It is also used to make someone feel like, or look like, a loser in order to give the critic an advantage. If you have the advantage you are a winner.

Criticism, even if it is untrue or unfair can still be damaging, 'throw enough mud and some will stick' is something we have all seen. Politics is a grand example of that tactic. A more subtle technique is used in advertising. The idea is to make us feel that we would be better off if we had their product or service. This is a covert criticism that your life is not as good as it could be or should be. Without their product you are a loser.

Criticism highlights that you are not good enough and if you are not good enough you are a failure and if you are a failure you are not able to be a success and if you are not able to be a success you have little to offer your family, your community, your workplace or even your country or the world and if you have little to offer then maybe you shouldn't be here. This disastrous spiral into a feeling of worthlessness destroys self-esteem and is definitely driving people crazy.

Here are some of the thoughts that cause emotional stress due to criticism:

- It is unacceptable to make a mistake.
- Don't ever let anyone know what goal you're working on. That way they won't consider you a failure if you don't reach it.
- Why doesn't anyone ever say anything good about me?
- Everyone says I have so many problems. I might as well give up right now.
- I am so dumb. I can never solve anything as complex as this.
- I've seen all the magazine covers and I know I am the ugliest, most unappealing, fat slob in the world.
- After what they said about me, I guess I must be uncreative, ineffective, and untalented.
- I'm never satisfied. I always think that I could do better.
- I just want Dad to be proud of me and say I did good. Just once.
- She's become such a bitch. At me all the time. I only tell her she's ugly to shut her up.

6. ISOLATION

This is a demon by stealth. Separation and disconnection are essential elements of the winner/loser world. Isolation is a feeling you get while living in the winner/loser world. It is like when you are in the water, you feel wet; when you are outside in the snow without a jacket, you feel cold; when you are in the dark and hear spooky noises you feel scared; so, when you live in a system that rewards you for being a separate, individual winner, which you can only do on your own, and punishes you for losing by separating you from winners then, whether you are a winner or a loser, you can feel isolated.

As we have already discussed, the winner/loser world is based on the concept of separate, individual endeavour. Although you may connect with other individuals, perhaps even operate as a team, there are greater rewards for a single winner and so there is always some motivation for division. Interaction is mostly by transaction and sometimes people who contribute to a winning result are denied recognition and any share of the spoils. I often encounter people who are distressed because they have been cut out of something and feel left out and isolated. Families argue and cut relatives out; scientific research only carries the names of a select few; friends will give someone the cold shoulder; children will not play with an unpopular or new child at school; 'tall poppies' are cut down as a punishment for success; prejudice aligns one group against another... and the examples could go on.

Human beings naturally require relationship and connection. We find isolation emotionally disturbing. This emotional disturbance makes us look weak in the winner/loser world. You feel and look like a loser and this isolates you more. It is a vicious cycle, and happens whether you are a winner or a loser. Isolation is the inescapable Catch-22 of the winner/loser world.

Here are some of the thoughts that cause emotional stress due to isolation:

- Nobody loves me.
- Unless I am 'Number One' there is no sense in trying. Everyone knows what 'Number Two' is. To win is the only acceptable goal.

- No one really likes a winner
- People are out to get all they can from you, so avoid them to survive.
- As soon as you let your guard down, you will be stepped on again!
- No one is to be trusted!
- You always get hurt by the ones you love!
- I get no respect from anyone!
- All men (or women) are dishonest and are never to be trusted! No matter.
- As soon as you care and open up to someone, they will always leave you!
- It is better to live alone for the rest of my life than to risk being hurt as I was!

7. GUILT

Guilt is a feeling that overcomes you when you believe you are responsible for things or you are made to believe you are responsible. We feel guilty when we fail, when we lose, when we regret past events, when we don't respond the way we should, when we are unable to please and live up to expectations, when someone else is suffering from failure or regret, when we choose the wrong actions, when what we do causes someone else to suffer and when it is our fault. That's enough for now!

Guilt grasps you and smothers you. Surely you can avoid guilt if you are a winner? We know the answer to that. I've heard it myself, "I'm doing really well, so why do I feel guilty?" Guilt is about feeling responsible for all the things that go wrong or even might go wrong. In the winner/loser world it is very difficult for anything to go completely right. Between the 8 Differences and the 7 Demons it is virtually inevitable that something will make you feel like you have lost. Guilt absolutely guarantees this.

Here are some of the thoughts that cause emotional stress due to guilt:

- I do not deserve to be happy
- I am responsible for my partner's happiness.
- There is only one 'right' way to do things.
- It is my fault if others in my life are not happy.
- If my kids fail, it's my responsibility.
- It is wrong to be concerned about myself.
- I must be vigilant to be sure I don't do something evil or wrong.
- I must always be giving to others.
- No matter what I do, I am always wrong.
- I should never feel guilty.
- If I do feel guilty, it's because I am or have been wrong.

In the winner/loser world, the only way to not be affected by all this is to not be affected at all, by anything. You can shut your emotions down, or keep them at a very shallow level. You can keep very busy or focus your energy on the competition of success. You can live for the moment, remembering nothing of yesterday and caring nothing about tomorrow. You can find some belief that takes the responsibility and bears your guilt. You can build an island around yourself and refuse to participate.

Or you can stare the winner/loser world in the face, know it for what it is and what it does, take the 'red pill' and step out into the Creative World. In an instant, guilt disappears, blame disappears, bad results cease to exist, isolation is impossible, criticism changes to helpful information and we become a participant in the creative experience of life.

With this change comes a whole new way of dealing with everything. You will invent and create and resolve in a million different ways. Many will be unique to you. They will be your own creation. But with any change comes a period of adjustment and settling. You will need some ready-made techniques and skills to use during this process. I have devised 6 practical exercises. These may well be all you need to escape the winner/loser world and enjoy the creative world. When you practice these techniques you will be able to respond to your experiences in a creative world way; you will also be able to function within the winner/loser world, but from the creative world perspective. (This may help you understand the old expression "I am in this world, but not of it". You can be 'in' the winner/loser world, but you are 'of' or from the creative world). Lastly, these exercises will allow you to quickly check any problem you are having and show whether you have slipped back into winner/loser ways.

Incorporate the 6 Practices into your daily life and the creative world is yours forever.

♦♦♦ THE 6 PRACTICES ♦♦♦

Thoughts can influence the brain: the software changes the hardware.

Dr Ernest Rossi

No matter how well you grasp a new idea it is still necessary to learn new behaviours and unlearn old habits. Based on the knowledge we have about neuronal pathways and memory building in the brain, it takes about three weeks to build and strengthen a new way of thinking, at the same time the old pathway weakens. Practical exercises and a structured program are very important to assist you in this process.

The most obvious and simple thing to do is to stop and ask yourself, "Am I doing a winner/loser world thing?" This seems so straightforward that I haven't included it in the group of six, but it is often the place to start when you are falling into the unhappy, stressful, argumentative, self defeating behaviours of the winner/loser world. The main 6 Practices, however, take you much further than a simple awareness check. Each exercise will reveal the creative world and all the benefits that come with it.

One more thing that is worth mentioning is that I believe everyone can benefit from participating in some type of acting class. That is not to say that everyone should be an actor or that everyone can be. Acting is simply a wonderful way to participate in the experience of shared interaction and creativity. It's not about whether you are good at it, it's about having the opportunity to let go of the winner/loser world and share a new experience within the safety of the play or improvisation or whatever. If you really can't get into the play-acting thing, then perhaps you might prefer to join a choir or something similar. The important thing is to make a contribution to a group activity that is enriched by your participation where the outcome is not concerned with winning or being better than something or being good enough. Just participate.

But that is just my belief. That does not mean I am 'right'. You may be inspired to want to do something completely different that lifts you to great heights. Bravo. Have a go!

Having given you those two overall activities, we can now focus on the specific and detailed exercises that provide a practical platform to the creative world program. First is the list, followed by their explanations.

1. **THE PROBLEM IS A MESSAGE**
2. **THAT'S INTERESTING**
3. **WHAT CAN I CREATE**
4. **TELL ME EVERYTHING IN YOUR HEAD**

5. THE PRIORITY TRIANGLE

6. RANDOM INSPIRATION

1. THE PROBLEM IS A MESSAGE

> *A problem is something you have to stop for and fix.*
> *A message is something that tells you what you need*
> *and points to where you can go.*

In the winner/loser world a problem is something that needs to be fixed. When something is 'wrong' it needs to be made 'right'. A problem is a barrier to progress. We have to stop for a problem. It disrupts your connection with others and affects your inner emotional health. We often say, "I can't do so-and-so until I solve this problem." Relationships go on hold; the way we behave toward other people can change; our confidence can be affected; and we can become preoccupied while problems are being solved. Problems at work interrupt life at home and problems at home can interrupt work. It's all about being *troubled.*

In the creative world a problem is something very different. A problem is an indicator or a symptom of something that we are not clearly aware of or that we are not noticing. The immediate problem is rarely the real issue. A problem is an opportunity and an inspiration to discover the underlying issue.

We get stuck in the problem because the winner/loser world focuses on fault/blame and other problems that come from a bad result. When we are consciously aware of a problem the solution seems to be to simply fix it.

The trouble is that our conscious awareness is, in fact, only aware on a very limited level. Because of this we process most of what is happening around us non-consciously (remember the processes involved in playing tennis). All we need to know in our conscious awareness is enough to help us survive. This is most often a vast simplification of what is really happening throughout your bodily systems and emotional needs.

Case example: When we become consciously aware of the problem that we are hungry there are a host of non-conscious processes involved that deal with a wide variety of detailed body actions (see the inset box). Hunger is easily fixed by eating, but there are other issues that may not be immediately apparent. Feeling hungry can be the courier of many different messages.

Hunger can be because we have an infection and there is a need for particular vitamins; we may need extra energy and so, we need to eat carbohydrates; we may be depressed about a relationship and we are seeking pleasure food; we may be trying to become too thin and be heading toward anorexia or bulimia; we may be taking drugs that cause us to feel hungry; we may be nervous about something we have to do; we may be punishing ourselves emotionally by over-eating. These are just some of the deeper issues that can be involved in the simple problem of feeling hungry even though hunger is so easily fixed by eating something. In fact the real issue may be best resolved by *not* eating. The real message can only come out if all the elements available are allowed to interact and produce an outcome.

The Non-Conscious Process of Digestion

Throughout the day our bodies are affected by a series of changes: our blood glucose levels change; there are also changes in cholecystokinin, insulin and glucagon; our body heat may drop; circadian rhythms enact learned behaviour patterns; smells affect our olfactory system; the volume of material in our stomach and intestine changes; the stomach can have contractions; the lateral hypothalamus responds to messages through the vagus nerve; and the paraventricular hypothalamus considers nutrient needs; we continuously process a variety of emotional states; social conditions present; and the body assesses its amount of leptin. All this extraordinary activity occurs completely outside of your conscious awareness. The body automatically creates the necessary and required responses to these changes. In this wonderfully complex process there is a point when there is a need for some conscious action. The way in which the body gains the attention of the conscious awareness is to create an emotional imperative. We become concerned about our sense of wellbeing. We have a need. An awareness of the true complexity of the situation would probably just create confusion, so we only become aware of the overall picture. All the genius of our conscious mind becomes aware of is a very simplistic problem - *I'm hungry*. We have a number of these simplistic realisations that affect our general behaviour: *I'm tired* - we go to sleep; *I'm sick* – we lie down and rest; *I'm unhappy* – we examine our feelings. The trouble is, in the 'real world', we stay awake because there is so much to do; we soldier on when we are sick; and we treat our emotional health as an embarrassment and pretend to be happy.

So, when your conscious mind becomes aware of a problem, it is because your non-conscious is trying to draw your attention to something that is blocking or disturbing your healthy and happy existence: the problem is an indicator of a deeper message. Strangely enough the words that describe the problem can often be the same as the message, but a problem is something to fix whereas a message is something to accept and create with.

Case examples:
Jenny: Jenny was stressed out of her mind because of her upcoming exam. It was too difficult for her and she believed she would not be able to cope. How could we solve this problem? The message was the same as the problem – "it is too difficult". Taking that as a truth, what was she trying to tell herself? This is not a very clear message. It's very general. Is everything too difficult? If not everything, then what is? What is the 'it' that is too difficult?

The first message is that the situation is being oversimplified and generalised. Jenny is not distinguishing between the exam and the many different situations involved in her current experience. The message is not that "everything is difficult", but that some things are difficult and that they are dominating the whole experience. During our sessions, Jenny looked deeper into her feelings and found that the only real problem was everybody's expectations of how well she should do. That is a huge winner/loser world pressure. We decided there was no problem because all she could do was her best. In fact, all the worry about whether she would do well was interfering with her ability to do her best. She understood that she would be able to create something with whatever result she achieved.

Paul: Paul was very sick. His illness was life threatening. Surely that is a problem and a message? Not to Paul. He saw a message in his illness. He saw the damage he and others had done to his body and his emotions. He recognised them as blocks and barriers to his wellbeing. The message of the illness was to clear these blocks and barriers and free himself from the weakness that had been created within him. He revisited the events of his life that hung around his neck like millstones and he discovered the lessons and the benefits. Then he was able to cut the events free. He shed their burden. There was no point trying to recover from his illness first and *then* work on his personal issues. He had no guarantee that he would recover at all, so he listened to the message and proceeded with his 'cure'. He took himself down fascinating and illuminating paths. He made changes and his wellbeing was revitalised. He became his own inspiration and an inspiration for many others. The illness still took him, but he left with a lighter heart. He was my best friend.

2. THAT'S INTERESTING.

The world is full of information and every bit of it is interesting.

In the creative world everything around you is information that you can add to the creative process of your experience. Everything that is said or done, whatever is happening, objects, feelings, sensations and anything else is information. Information is interesting. A healthy creative world response to any and all information is, "That's interesting".

It's interesting because something new can come of it. The information may be in the form of a problem, so that is interesting because of the message. Everything has the opportunity to teach and inspire.

Case example: George was constantly bothered by a co-worker, Barry, who would regularly criticise him. "You should have finished high school, George." "You shouldn't put up with how your girlfriend carries on." "Why don't you buy a house and stop renting? You're just wasting money" and so on.

George was ready to give Barry a punch in the head. Barry made George feel like he was doing the wrong thing (being a loser) and had to defend himself. Instead, we decided to try the *that's interesting* approach. Whenever Barry made a comment George would respond with, "That's interesting." Not as a cynical or critical remark, but because it was *actually* interesting.

George was able to see that Barry's stupid comments were actually giving him the opportunity to consider whether he was saying something beneficial. How about going back to high school? Well, as George was about to qualify as a first class tradesman there was no need to have a high school qualification, but maybe there were some things that George enjoyed in high school that he'd like to try again. It might be interesting to do a few courses on weekends or at night. George found that he was actually able to sincerely say, "Gee, thanks for the idea, Barry."

It was also interesting that Barry thought that George needed his advice. Maybe he was having a hard time at home and no one was listening to him, or he had to compete with a domineering parent. What's really interesting is that Barry didn't seem to mind if George thought he was an overbearing twerp. Maybe Barry needed someone to talk to with a sympathetic ear. Maybe the problem of Barry was a message from Barry that he needed to feel useful and desperately wanted someone to listen to him. That is all very interesting and very helpful, and has created a whole raft of new possibilities for George and Barry.

3. WHAT CAN I CREATE?

> *When you give up the distracting game of winning and losing,*
> *you are left with the exciting prospect of what you can create.*

This is a wonderfully simple exercise and is the one that can be used in every situation at some point. When you are confronted with a situation that disturbs you there are three simple steps. You know that something is disturbing because you are affected in a negative emotional way that makes you feel lesser. The best indication is when you feel down, like you are a loser, like you don't know what to do, exasperated, tired, you feel cranky or defensive.

Step 1 is to ask yourself, "What am I trying to win?"

Step 2 is to ask yourself, "What am I afraid of losing?"

Unless you are under some direct threat to your personal safety you can just push the winning and losing stuff aside. For example, if you are thinking about the 10 tonne truck that is driving toward you, then the last thing you should be doing is thinking. In fact, your body would have taken over long ago and you would have flung yourself out of the way. You may be lying in the dirt worried about being embarrassed or whether you have torn your new trousers or whether everyone is thinking you are an idiot, but none of these things matter compared with being hit by the 10 tonne truck! Hopefully there is no truck and just winner/loser world thoughts, so we can go to the third step.

Step 3 is to ask yourself, "What can I create out of this situation?"

Now, you simply let your imagination play with the possibilities and allow new outcomes to emerge. This will change the situation completely. Continue to do this until you create something you can work with. Include everything possible: what is happening; what you want; what you need; restrictions that are unavoidable; possible ways to avoid the restrictions. Even the answers you gave in the first two steps should be included. Remember: everything is information and all information is interesting because information expands the creative possibilities.

There are several ways for you to know when an outcome is desirable and when you have created something you want to work with.

Firstly, be aware of your emotions. If you feel awful then your body is telling you that the outcome is not desirable. If you feel positive and a new sense of vigour then this is a creative direction you should follow. Don't get too complex or delve too deeply into these feelings. If more problems arise then utilise the *message in the problem* technique. Pay attention. Let your whole system communicate and allow yourself to notice what happens, not just what you think should happen or what you want to happen.

A **second way** is to ask people you know what *they* think of the situation and of the direction you are going. That doesn't mean you must do what they say, but if you respond positively to anything that is said you will create new and more desirable outcomes. Sometimes others can see things more clearly than we can. Sometimes others can find the right words for us. Sometimes people make comments that are so stupid you get a great message by default. Remember, any comments or reactions are simply wonderful pieces of information.

Thirdly, we can listen to the sounds we make. This is a linguistic technique that I have observed and developed over the past decade. See the inset box 'The Ahh Principle'. As you learn to listen to these sounds in yourself, you will discover an extremely powerful tool that allows you to quickly recognise how you are feeling.

The 'Ahh' Principle

You've possibly heard of an 'aha moment' and the 'Ahh' Principle is along those lines. There are, however, three sound responses that give great insight into how you feel about something. Each indicates a level and type of awareness.

There are three broad types of awareness: rational; emotive; and intuitive/resonant.

Rational acknowledgement is shown with – **uh huh, yep, okay** – often accompanied by a knowing nod of the head. This means that you are satisfied with the information; it makes sense to you and fits into what you are prepared to accept. It also has the proviso that all is well, until there is more information and then the opinion may change. So, it is an indication of potentially temporary, acceptance that satisfies your general thinking and/or state of mind.

Emotional discomfort is show with – **urrrr, erhh, urk** – often accompanied with a curling of the top lip and wrinkling of the nose as if there is a bad smell. This shows that there is an emotional reaction to the situation that has a negative and as yet unresolved nature. This is a great indicator of an unresolved winner/loser issue. This could be a persisting event, guilt, unresolved issues with family etc. This response invites some attention to find out what the emotional disturbance is.

The intuitive/resonant response is shown with –ahh, aha – always accompanied by an opening of the mouth and throat and a relaxing of the shoulders, possibly with an opening movement of the arms and hands. This happens when there is a deep series of associations not only in the conscious, thinking awareness, but in the non-conscious, innate sense of self. It marks a feeling of satisfaction and 'rightness' even if only for you, individually. It indicates that this is positive direction and a desirable outcome that will be beneficial if allowed to continue. This is right for you.

By creating something new you will escape the restraint of what you fear and become inspired and energised by what might come. *What can I create* is an exercise that gives you somewhere to go and evaporates any emotional distress. This doesn't mean that you become emotionless, quite the opposite, but any negative emotion that you had about the event is no longer possible because you have created a new outcome. You are no longer in the same event. Time has moved on. You are somewhere else in a new event and the past upsetting event (albeit fairly recent past) has ceased to exist except as a memory and as a source of valuable lessons. Wow.

Case example: Jessie didn't think that the magazines for teenage girls were very good. She wanted a magazine that discussed issues that were more challenging and political, not just how to be pretty for boys. So she decided to start her own. With a few friends she began this daunting task. Like all daunting tasks, there were many bumps along the way, but each time she bounced into the next step. When support waned she found greater leadership and determination within herself. She needed to. More to the point is that it happened to her anyway. When she needed money and there was none, she created new opportunities. She did this by believing that it was possible to find an investor (as different from probable). To her surprise, and to her credit, she found some investors and the project continued. When it proved impossible for her to produce all the content, instead of giving up she wondered what would happen if she put a request on the Internet. Material came in hand over fist. Eventually a publisher was needed and somehow found, but just before publication there were problems and the magazine was never produced. What a sad end to the story. Well, only if you think in results. Jessie looked for another outcome. Before long she applied for a job in the media business, but found that she was up against people with university degrees. When she was asked what she could do, Jessie put the demonstration copy of her magazine on the table. They hired her. That company went bust and Jessie is looking for employment again. Her job applications are very inventive because of all the things she has been able to learn. I even suggested she might have a great book in development – *101 Fascinating Job Applications.* Who knows? What we do know is that whatever was the last thing she did, will be the springboard that she can use for the next thing. It's not about *not* giving up, it is realising that you *can't* give up – your inner creative capacity won't let it. One thing always leads to another. That is, unless you allow the winner/loser world to box you in with failure and disappointment.

4. TELL ME EVERYTHING IN YOUR HEAD.

You cannot create a rainbow with only half the colours of the spectrum. The only way to truly share is to share everything, leaving nothing to guesswork

One of the biggest problems in the winner/loser world is that everything is tempered by concerns about winning and losing. That is not to say that in the creative world you should be blithely frank and open with everyone and anyone. The winner/loser world definitely exists and all too few people are aware of the creative world. So, it may not be safe to be open with some people. Caution is not unwise. The trouble is that we can get caught up in caution and get into bad winner/loser world habits. We protect ourselves by holding our thoughts back. This includes partners, families and friends where we should be open and trusting. Instead these relationships are limited by a shortage of information.

Relationships suffer enormously from this partial sharing of what is in our head. The fear of being defeated or damaged in some way is not a healthy component in any relationship. I hear it so often, "He/she should know that without me having to tell them." "I gave him so many clues. He must be stupid to not know what I wanted." "I don't know what she wants. I just keep doing a bunch of things and see if she looks a bit happier." "Why don't my staff understand how hard it is at the moment?" "Mum and Dad are down on me about something. Dunno what it is, but it's probably something stupid."

We seem to expect some sort of magic understanding of our needs and wants. Somehow we expect people to know when we need and how we want it without any clear information at all. The exercise of *tell me everything in your head* cuts out the guesswork. You literally tell them everything that is in your head. Then all the information is out in the open and the creative process can continue without limitation.

Be aware, though, this exercise is a creative world exercise. In the winner/loser world you can't share what's in your head because of right and wrong, fault and blame and criticism. These demons come out to undermine what is said and destroy creative opportunity. Even in the creative world we have another difficulty: language. Language is a wonderful mechanism for communication, but it is full of frailties and inconsistencies. Any communication runs a very high risk of being misunderstood. Just because you have said something does not mean that the other person will clearly understand.

Just because you have used a word the way you usually use it does not mean that that is the way the other person uses it. Just because you have uttered a word to express your inner thought doesn't mean that word is the best choice. Language needs to be worked with and played with until both parties are satisfied that the communication is clear and successful.

If you can't find the right word then I suggest that you play around with the possibilities. Just say any word or words that you can or that seem to relate to the situation and use that as a springboard or a stepping-stone toward the discovery of a word that satisfies. That is the same principle as with outcomes. Don't demand a result. Work with the outcomes (what is said) until there is understanding. If every word you utter is supposed to be a good result, speaking becomes very cautious and tedious. Just look at politicians and lawyers. On the other hand, if words that you utter are stepping stones down the creative path of communication – which is the same as connection and interaction – then speaking becomes an acceptably fallible process. It is just horrible when you are tied to words you have said and they are used as weapons to make you fail.

When you use language as a process of connection it is safe to share everything in your head. Remember the artist and the colours on the palette? If you only put half the colours in your head on their palette and then expect others to paint with all the light and shade you imagine, then you can only end up being disappointed. Communication is nigh on impossible when you impose the guessing game.

Case example: Sally was convinced that her husband, Alan, was stupid. He never knew what she wanted or when she wanted it. She had been reading a few books about how men were insensitive and didn't understand women. She felt vindicated, but what could she do about it?

I asked her to talk about an example or two. On one occasion he had a business function that she didn't want to go to. She said she would, but it was annoying that they had to waste a night out on business. She felt the people at his work were shallow and self-seeking. Although she resigned herself to going, she decided that she didn't have anything to wear and needed to buy something. It was his fault for making her go in the first place. He couldn't understand why she needed something new. Surely he could see that every time the function was mentioned she was unhappy. Still, he flatly refused to let her spend money unnecessarily. It turned into a huge persistent fight. Sally went out and bought some new things anyway and he hit the roof.

After a number of sessions to wade through this seemingly simple issue we were finally able to reveal the full story. Alan was totally baffled that Sally had never wanted to go to the function. As far as he was concerned she said it was okay and that was that. She was totally amazed that he couldn't see that her dissatisfaction with her wardrobe was clearly showing that she didn't want to go. Couldn't he hear the tone of her voice? Another problem was that Alan was worried about their finances. He had heard through the office grapevine that the bonuses for that year were not going to be as large as usual. He hadn't told Sally because it wasn't official, but if he said they couldn't afford it then she should believe him.

As all this information began to emerge they both began to soften. They soon realised that it was all a huge misunderstanding. Now, I wasn't going to let them get away with that. It wasn't a huge misunderstanding, it was a deliberate game based on keeping the higher moral ground. The fact that neither Sally nor her husband had a clear idea of the true situation was ignored in the effort to place blame. It had to be the other person's fault and so they blamed each other for being insensitive, stupid, untrusting and unreliable.

Just tell someone everything that is in your head and you can, by interacting respectfully and caringly, create a peaceful and mutually satisfying outcome. Well, at least an outcome that is going to be a lot better than playing truth tug-of-war. Sally and Alan eventually agreed.

5. THE PRIORITY TRIANGLE

At the top of the triangle of your life is the reason why you bother doing anything below it.

In the creative world, unless you are dealing with a situation that is directly and immediately concerning your survival, there is no need to have winning as your first priority. Your first priority is the enjoyment of your relationships and interactions. This is how you create an environment of peace and happiness. Put simply, being alive, loving your partner, playing with the kids, sharing with friends, caring for others are the things we all want to do because that make us feel good. So often, when people have near death experiences or some other tragic threat to life, they talk about 'getting their priorities right' and focussing on relationships, connection and caring.

Let's cut out the middleman and not wait until death rattles our door to set these priorities. There is a very simple exercise to show what is at the top of your priorities. Imagine a triangle and at the top there is a cherry (you can have a blob of cream on it if you wish). Imagine that this cherry is the relationship, connected, caring parts of your life. The triangle may be full of various things that need to be done, but none is more important than the cherry and all it stands for. Imagine that for a moment or two.

Now, let's return to the real world (yes, that is a joke – ish) and think about all the things that you have to get done right now. Think about the pressures, the responsibilities, the mortgage, the guy down the street who just got a new car, the woman at the office who has clearly had plastic surgery, the mess in the backyard, the mountain of clothing in the ironing basket, etc. You know what I mean.

Now that I have dumped you squarely back in the winner/loser world, I want you to think about the next set of questions. First, draw a triangle on a piece of paper or on a whiteboard. Now, write the answers into this new triangle: 1. Which things have to be done first before you can feel free to relax? 2. What has to be done first before you can let go of some of your stress? 3. What do you need to get off your plate before you can get together with your mates? 4. What do you have to get right in your life before you can deal with your partner's needs? 5. How much time do you need to wind down from the grind of work before you can deal with the kids? I expect that your triangle is probably quite full.

Where is the cherry?

I'll bet you that it is not on the top any more, if anywhere at all. What you are seeing now is the winner/loser world triangle. Sitting at the top is a wizened old prune that represents getting things done, satisfying the needs of the 'real world', keeping everyone else happy, not being at fault or to blame – in short, battling to not lose. That is the priority of the winner/loser world triangle. "As soon as I can get this done I'll be able to show my feelings and share some time with you". That may sound okay, but if you never get it all done and never get to the finish line, then the prune stays on top. In the winner/loser world the finish line is constantly moving.

So let's return to the creative world triangle where the cherry is back on top.

In this exercise, make a list of the things that the cherry represents. Don't make it too detailed, just the great feelings, important people and the important things you enjoy doing. Then, imagine you are in the presence of these people or able to do any of the things that are important. Notice whether you connect and enjoy or whether you are still distracted by the other 'stuff'. If you find you *are* distracted then you are still in the winner/loser world triangle. Something must be done.

I am not saying that you give up work, stop paying the mortgage and ignore your social responsibilities while you cuddle your partner, play with the kids and let everything fall apart. That is one of those 'drop out of the world' systems. I am saying that you can do all the things you need to do in the 'real world' AND cuddle your partner, play with kids and enjoy your life. The problem is that the 'real world stuff' is allowed to block our ability to connect and we don't cuddle our partner, even when they are standing right in front of us – we're too tired. We don't play with the kids, even when we can – we're too stressed. We don't create connection in the moments that we can because we are too disconnected as we struggle to get results - to win. In fact, the struggle is mostly an effort against losing. In the winner/loser world we spend more time at the losing end of the scale than the winning end.

Back to the creative world. Where is the cherry? That is the question to ask again and again and again until the cherry rises and stays on top. Keep putting the 'stuff' you have to do down into the triangle and push the cherry to the top.

Case example: Frank was engaged to Janine. Everything was alright, but they would regularly find themselves arguing. It was always about something different, so Frank didn't see that there was a particular problem, but he didn't want the arguing to continue. They didn't argue all the time. Sometimes they would just get... heated.

One night they planned to meet at the railway station and through a comedy of errors he was waiting in the car while she waited on the platform. When they finally worked it out they were both upset. They played the blame game for a while and then gave each other the silent treatment. End result was definitely not a romantic evening. Another time Frank was working on a business project on his computer and Janine kept asking questions about dinner. Finally, he told her to stop asking things and she told him to stop expecting to be waited on hand and foot. Romance went out the window again. There was a whole host of these types of stories.

I drew a triangle on the whiteboard and we put the cherry on top. I asked him what had to be done before he was able to relax. If it was important and had to be done first it went into the triangle with the highest priority at the bottom. Soon we had a triangle full of 'stuff' with a cherry on top. I then asked him whether he felt the image on the whiteboard rang true. Frank screwed up his brow and said he wasn't really sure. So, I turned the whiteboard upside down, which put the point of the triangle at the bottom. Now the most important things to be done were at the top, but the cherry was not looking very happy at the bottom. Frank got the message. "That's more like the truth," he exclaimed. He was shocked. When we put the cherry on the top of the upright triangle he was sure that he was doing the right thing. He knew he loved her and wanted everything to be great for them both. Unfortunately, he didn't know how to do that before all the 'stuff' got done.

I turned the whiteboard around again and suggested that rather than enjoying the cherry *after* getting everything done, what about getting everything done *because* of their love and happiness, which was symbolised by the cherry. That meant Frank could enjoy Janine *while* he was doing what he had to do. It had never occurred to him that you could do the 'stuff' of life at the same time that you enjoyed yourself.

6. RANDOM INSPIRATION

The vital piece of information you need is being played out before you in the events of your life. With practice you will be able to see beyond the literal and delve into the inspiring message.

Edward De Bono explained the principle behind this exercise decades ago. He called it 'lateral thinking' and I strongly suggest you read everything he has written about our creative capacity. However, I think we can take the idea a few steps further.

One of the most amazing outcomes of the creative nature of human beings is that we are able to see the world not only in its literal form, but we are also able to imagine things that the literal thing represents or symbolises. We are inspired by the literal to become conscious of other things. These 'other things' are usually specifically relevant to what you *need* to realise or will benefit you to realise. This means that inherent in the creative process, that is continuously operating, your needs as an individual are the most important element. Your needs and wants are the foundation platform for everything that happens. Because the greater majority of our creative interaction is non-conscious (remember the story of feeling hungry) there is a lot going on within us that has not been given a voice. Lateral thinking, or responding to symbolic representations, can bring a non-conscious 'knowing' into our conscious awareness. That means that we can consciously act to help and focus the process of bringing things into our awareness. You will know this has happened when you can put it into words and it excites the 'ahh principle'. Simply, when we can say it, we can do it. These words are often inspired by the process of symbolic reference arising from the literal events that surround us.

For example, you see an eagle and you might think about freedom; you open the fridge door and you might imagine adventuring to the North Pole; you dream of a snake swallowing its own tail and you suddenly wake up with the solution to the chemical formula of boron (true story).

If you think you are still having some trouble with how this works (or that it does work at all!) then consider this: over the last few minutes you have imagined an eagle, a fridge, the North Pole and a self-cannibalistic snake. You did all this from the symbolic representations created by a bunch of squiggles on the page in front of you called 'written words'. Just to be sure though, quickly look around now for any eagles, fridges, snowstorms or snakes!

So, the trick is getting the relevant messages from your intuitive or non-conscious awareness into words. You can do this through the inspiration of ordinary day-to-day events. This is a very creative act and, like all creative acts, you will improve with practice. The skill, however, is not in *how* to create the realisation because that comes naturally. The skill is to learn how to *notice* it and *recognise* it when it comes.

We are already assisted by the simple 'rule of thumb' technique – the 'Ahh Principle'. This helps us notice how we feel about communications from our non-conscious. The 'Ahh Principle' is one of the central mechanisms that enable us to notice, realise and recognise. Enlisting this 'noticing device', practice your skills with the following methods. You might use them separately or together. Remember, there is no single 'right' way, just an interactive, creative way.

1) Entertain whatever comes into your head.
Don't look for what makes sense. You must allow for any possibility. Creative thought often doesn't make any sense at first, but after a little thought the logical rationale can fall into place. Sometimes the information that supports the idea is not readily available. It might take some time to come across the information that makes sense of your creative vision. In that case the idea will just sit in the background waiting. The

important thing is that the idea was allowed to exist, rather than rejected for lack of logic or sensibility.

2) Listen to your body.

Messages can manifest in lots of ways as they endeavour to find their expression in words. You may feel sensations like aches, pains or even tingles somewhere on your body. You may have an unusual or seemingly unwarranted emotional response. You may feel nervous or excited or defensive or other feelings of concern. If these sensations are strong enough to notice then you may well be getting a message from your body. Allow yourself to respond and see what you are inspired to imagine. See what it makes you think of. If that thought is relevant and helpful then you are paying attention.

3) Take some time.

It may certainly be that your realisation is like a flash of light and is suddenly overwhelming, but more often than not it can take some time for everything to sink in and make sense. Let your mind play with the outcome of any realisation because it may just be a stepping-stone to the heart of your need.

4) Use a tool.

De Bono made the suggestion that just opening the dictionary and putting your finger on a word can send your mind thinking in unusual directions. These directions only seem unusual because we tend to think in the same pattern (along strong neural pathways). Lateral thinking is just the process of letting the mind shoot off in other directions. This is a much more accurate reflection of the way out neurons are wired together. Every neuron is connected in a multitude of different potential pathways.

The more symbolic the tool, the more inspirational it can be. A sentence will give you more than just a word. The sentence can help to create context. I have found that the more the tool relates to our symbolic history the better. Passages that have reference to mythology or with strong pictorial reference can be very inspiring. Remember, though, these tools are inspiring you to discover words that describe an awareness you already possess, but which need to get out of the non-conscious (right-brain) and into words.

The best words are heralded by the 'Ahh' response. To that end, there are a number of symbolic tools that can inspire you. Some are used in the esoteric community. Things like the I Ching or the Runes can be very good, although I find that their symbolic references are too dated. The Sabian Symbols are an excellent modern set of verbal symbolic pictures. Even things like tarot cards and other pictorial cards can be very helpful. I still have a lot of questions about the fortune telling side of these tools, but as inspirational tools to engender conscious verbal awareness, they can be terrific. The way I think we should use these sorts of tools is with the clear understanding that there is no 'magical' or 'mysterious' power that is doing anything. You don't need it. You are already a magical and mysterious power in yourself.

5) Let the mind play.
The right words are not easy to find, despite the blasé attitude most of us have toward language. Our language skills have still got a long way to go on the evolutionary level. It is no accident that there are very few great authors. If language and communication were easy then you would expect there to be many more. Is it hard for you to find the best words to describe how you feel? The task can be very frustrating. The best thing to do is to let lots of words out into the air so that you have more options. The 'Ahh Principle' will often point out the best choice or, at least, the best stepping-stones.

5) Share the thoughts
Talk about your thoughts and feelings with others. If they are willing, it is a great way to get a broader appreciation of what you are trying to notice. The expression on someone's face as you tell them a story can be an instant clue to their reaction.

Other people can act as mirrors to our own experience. Their feedback can be just the trigger toward some extra clarity. We see it all the time in plays where the character who is trying to work something out is inspired by some seemingly meaningless thing said or done by someone else. It is entertaining drama, but also very true to life.

Example: These examples come from a series of pieces I wrote called 'Life Tips'. They are just little stories that I saw in my day-to-day life, which led me to a clearer and stronger awareness of a deeper philosophy or life skill.

Waiting:
How much time do we spend waiting? Waiting for that job; waiting for a pay rise; waiting till we can afford it; waiting for retirement; waiting for that stroke of luck. When I visited Lake Geneva in Switzerland I made plans to take a ferry tour. I woke early, only to find that a thick fog had settled in. I had to wait, so I wandered around to the public park on the shore and sat down, just, sort of, killing time. Then I thought, "What am I doing with my head in my hands? I'm on the shores of Lake Geneva!" So I looked around. There was a young family on the small sandy beach and they were beset by a flock of swans that emerged from the mist looking for easy food. Several sailboats ploughed into the mist like it was a series of translucent gauze curtains that floated back behind them as they dissolved out of sight. Up on the grass was a couple that *needed* some gauze curtains - to cover up. And I nearly missed all this, with my head in my hands ... waiting. Participate in the world while you wait and you no longer 'kill time'. Remember the time you kill is called life-time.

Chris:
My friend Chris had a heart attack last year. I hadn't seen him for years, but there he was, sitting in my kitchen over a cup of tea telling me about his life, his heart and his new adventure. He'd asked his heart specialist what prescription would keep

him healthy and the doctor told him, "Go and be happy". Being in my kitchen was the first step in getting away. He is such an intelligent man. He even won a big money quiz show some years ago, but lost it all on bad business, bad marriage and bad management. He'd been trying to get away from himself for years, but his clogged up arteries convinced him that he was who he was and that you can't get away from yourself. Now he was determined to make a start. So we sat in the kitchen sharing tea, old stories and a few thoughts on Plato and Descartes. In truth, we were both making a fresh start, but it was not about getting away. It was about going *somewhere*. As the doctor said, "go and be happy". That's where I'm going - to be happy.

♦♦♦ THE WINNER/LOSER WORLD PROBLEM ♦♦♦

Society has evolved from the foundation of being an inattentive, unresponsive parent while it pursues the task of controlling the group.

Richard Hill

The winner/loser world problem is so fundamental to understanding why the world is going crazy that I want to give one more metaphor for easier understanding. You may also find it helpful to have a visual description after so much reading.

As I described earlier, the winner/loser world problem is the frustration that occurs when we are torn between the human need and desire for connection, and the winner/loser world demand for separate endeavour and competition. As each 'necessity' pulls at us we become highly vulnerable to stress, unhappiness and feel the inevitable doom of some impending failure.

To help get a physical sense of this frustration I want you to do a simple exercise. Hold your hands up in front of you. Face your palms toward you and your fingers pointing to the ceiling. Wiggle your fingers. This represents the separated experience of the winner/loser world.

Now, lightly interlock your fingers together so that your hands are in a clasped praying position in front of you. Gently wiggle your fingers together. Feel each finger as they move against each other. Each individual finger is experiencing the opportunity of interacting with the finger on either side of it. This represents the interaction of the creative world.

We don't have a problem, yet. The problem is caused when we try to hold the fingers in both positions at once. You simply cannot have the fingers interlocked AND separated at the same time. Whenever the fingers are separated they want to become interlocked and when they are interlocked there is a pressure for them to separate – at least during this exercise.

So, interlock your fingers and then pull your fingers apart. Now interlock your fingers again and this time, resist them being pulled apart. Finally your fingers will separate because if you resist too much it will actually hurt. When your fingers are apart feel that there is a real need and even some benefit to be interlocked. Repeat the process of separating and interlocking with an increasing resistance to making a change.

It won't take long before you will have to stop because it is just too painful to continue and is beginning to be quite distressing on the fingers.

Because your fingers are hurting it feels better to hold your fingers in the separated position. This is just what happens in the 'real world'. Interaction with others can be difficult and upsetting, which leads us to believe that we are better off remaining separate and independent. The irony is that it is the winner/loser world that is making our interactions so painful. That is why separation is one of the demons – it gets inside the situation and plays games. Eventually we *choose* to do the very thing that will do us the most harm. It is a sting of criminal proportions.

So, the biggest irony of the winner/loser world problem is that we end up in the worst position and, yet, still believe that we've made the best choice. While we remain in the framework of the winner/loser world we will continue wanting to come together, but whenever we do we will eventually feel the need to break apart. We break by becoming so stressed our lives that we lose our minds or just give up. The winner/loser world problem needs to be removed before we break irreparably.

♦♦♦ DEALING WITH THE DIFFERENCES ♦♦♦

I hear and I forget. I see and I remember. I do and I understand.

Confucius

Now that we have gone through the process of creating the definitions and the creative world 'language' it is a good idea to revisit the Differences and the Demons in a more practical, experiential way. This is a discussion of ideas and of suggestions of what you can do. Please add your own notes and listen to your own suggestions. Remember, you're in the creative world now!

EXCLUSION / INCLUSION

Exclusion is a two edged sword. You can be excluded, or you can be the one that is doing the excluding. Either way, you end up being isolated and isolation disconnects you. When you are disconnected you are alone. No one wants that. Often we exclude ourselves or push others away as a form of self-punishment for some perceived failure. This satisfies the guilt demon. Sometimes exclusion is a self-protective act because of fear: fear of failure, fear for personal safety, fear of being hurt, and fear of hurting others.

The only way to combat exclusion is to include and allow yourself to be included. If you feel you simply can't overcome your fears, then you can try little things that might help shake you out of the winner/loser world. Going to a funny movie is a way of shifting your mood. When you laugh at the funny parts you are joining in something and including yourself in the humour. It doesn't matter that you may be sitting in the theatre on your own. Cooking is another inclusive process. You need to buy the food and interact with the people who work in the market and fruit shop. You will need to interact with the person who wrote the cookbook, even though they are only there in the directions of the recipe. Cook more than you need and, rather than waste good food, you may be motivated to ask someone to join you.

These sorts of simple activities that involve just a little bit of outer creative expression can remind you that you are connected and included. When you enter the creative experience you will find that the problem of exclusion disappears. Exclusion cannot exist in the creative world because creativity requires inclusion where the elements interact to create outcomes.

EVENTS / LESSONS - OPPORTUNITIES
When an event has caused a great deal of harm it can be very difficult to get away from it. We can feel haunted by its memory even when we know there is nothing that can be done to change it. Using *the problem is a message* helps to highlight the key issue: that there is nothing you can do to change an event. The first creatively intelligent thing to do is to acknowledge this.

The only lasting benefit from an event is what you learn. It is vital that you focus your attention on what you have learnt. It is so easy to wallow in an event where you were a loser and so easy to linger in an event where you were a winner. Either way you are stuck in the past and you are removed from the present.

It may be necessary to think about the event again to reconsider what you may have learnt. This might be difficult, especially if it was a painful event, but it can be done. If you are very troubled, then you are telling yourself that you need some help. You can talk to a caring friend or a professional. The important thing is to listen to yourself. Feeling uncomfortable or troubled is a message, not a failing. You may believe that what you have learnt just confirms that you are a loser: that you cannot trust; that you must protect yourself; that you can never win; that you don't need anyone. This is simply a powerful and insistent message to yourself that your head, and perhaps your heart, is stuck in the winner/loser world. Never resist the benefit of getting some help and some support. In the creative world you fix things by leaving the world of separation. Then you can create solutions through the process of connecting and interacting.

If you find that you feel overtaken by the event to the degree that you sometimes even believe you are back there again, then you might be suffering from post-traumatic stress disorder (PTSD). This inability to shake the effects of a past experience may first need some professional treatment for PTSD. When you have got your mind back into the right timeframe you will find that you can return to an examination of the lessons learnt.

The important focus is on what has been learnt and how you are applying that learning into your experience at the moment. If there is continued distress then you are just telling yourself that you are still focussing on the event. It is only where your life goes *because* of an event that matters. The clearer you are about that, the sooner you can step forward.

INSTRUCTION / INFORMATION

Being instructed can be difficult to avoid sometimes. This is because sometimes instruction is the only way that certain types of information can be revealed. Very often we need to follow instructions quite strictly in order to achieve creative freedom later. This type of instruction is concerned with the teaching of technique and current know-how. I know, for example, that playing a musical instrument is more than just letting go and being creatively free. There is, eventually, a time when you can do that, but there is a lot to know about how the instrument works first. You need to learn what you can do with the instrument and also what it can do with you!

Even though I didn't attend formal piano classes, I sought the advice of professional friends and they all pointed me to technical exercises. A brilliant jazz musician gave me a book of scales. To improvise I needed fingers that were strong, supple and that knew the keys well. I also renovated an old piano and got to know how it was built. This was very helpful for me, although I don't think that everyone has to do this. Then I practiced - a lot. Eventually I was able to freely interact (improvise) with the piano and now we make music together.

So, instruction is not a problem when it is information. Whenever you find instruction to be upsetting try to free yourself from the limitation of not wanting to be told. Overcome this limitation with the pressing urge to know. When you know more, you are more and more outcomes spontaneously manifest.

It can also be helpful to spend a little bit of time contemplating why you are setting up a barrier. Use the *what can I create?* exercise to help reveal your winner/loser fears. All information connects you and allows you to feel not only what is happening inside you, but also to feel what it might be like inside the people and things you are interacting with (see *Zen and the Art of Everything* in Section 2).

COMPETITION / INSPIRATION

This is a tricky one to deal with clearly. Being competitive is very natural and healthy, except when it starts to own your behaviour and dehumanise your relationships with others. The ends can never justify the means if the 'means' damage you or those around you.

To feel that you can do better is a very creative thing. To see someone else perform and imagine that you could do similar or better is a valuable inspiration. To become determined to make the current winner eat the bitter fruit of losing in the wake of your conquering domination is a bit sick. Unfortunately, there are a number of motivationalists who seem to teach that message. They may not admit to it, but that's what it boils down to in the end.

The secret of competition is to take your natural desire to express yourself fully and create an outcome. In the winner/loser world winning means that you have achieved your result and you have nothing else to achieve. Mostly you have to shift from achieving to defending the position you have won. In the creative world you may reach an outcome where you have won, but that is not the last possibility. What can you create from that? Even if you thought that winning was possible, perhaps you are now in a position to try what you had thought was *not* possible. You may even be able to do something you had never even thought about at all. That is what makes the creative world so inspiring and exhilarating. It is simply not the same as the basic drive of competition, which is so demanding, confronting and yet, limiting.

Some of the greatest moments in competition have come from acts that were expressions of connection and interaction. In 1956, at the Australian National Athletics Championships, John Landy was running in the mile event. He was the second man to break the 4-minute mile and he was keen to make a strong showing before the 1956 Olympics. Many believed that he was going to break the world record. Also running was the Australian junior mile champion, Ron Clarke. The race proceeded at a cracking pace and the world record was on. About halfway around the track, Clarke stumbled and fell. Landy jumped over him, but his spikes cut into Clarke's shoulder. After a few steps Landy stopped and returned to make sure Clarke was all right. Clarke urged Landy to stop worrying about him and run! Together they set off after the other runners. The other runners had continued to run and were 60 yards ahead. Clarke and Landy sprinted off for the second half of the mile.

The crowd shouted wildly as Landy hauled in the front-runners. He quickly ran round the rest of the field and came into the home straight, leaving Clarke behind. He stormed down the track and in the last ten yards passed the leaders to win the Australian Championship in four minutes and four seconds. He would clearly have broken the world record if he had not stopped. On his victory lap Landy received one of the greatest ovations in the history of sport. Stopping to pick up Clarke had cost him eight or ten seconds. But it also unleashed in him a finish that was beyond anything ever seen before. Even Landy wondered at the feat. Later, he went on to set several world records, but this day, when Landy instinctively reacted to his sense of connection, he claimed one of his greatest victories and athletic immortality.

There are many ways to compete and find personal victory without crossing the finish line first. In this story it is not only Landy who is remembered, but also Clarke who spurred Landy on to continue the race. Both men discovered something new within themselves that day, despite the fact that only one was able to finish the race first.

RESULT / OUTCOME

A result has a sense of finality about it. One of the biggest frustrations in working toward a result is that many of the steps along the way seem insufficient and almost interfering. In the creative world there will be outcomes that are momentous and feel more important than others, but it is the pleasure of each 'stepping stone' outcome along the way that makes the experience totally enjoyable.

We are encouraging of very young children whatever they achieve, but they are still quite young when the pressure starts to produce a winning result. I have seen children in primary school as young as eight and nine showing symptoms of frustration because they have not yet achieved their desired result: getting high marks; being chosen in the sports team; gaining their teacher's praise and attention. This is not to say that no one should have goals. Goals are a great way to establish direction and maintain focus. It is, however, the journey that constructs our life, not the jerky movement from one goal to the next. Our journey may even lead to unexpected goals. That is the way of the creative world.

It may be easier to shift from result to outcome. It is a little more difficult, I expect, to discover how to be fascinated and excited at every step along the way. This, of course, takes practice and support. Some say that this step-by-step focus will slow everything down and make final achievement impossible. To that, I must say that I find things move quicker. The energy of fascination and excitement propels the whole process forward. On the other hand, what's the rush?

PROBABILITY / POSSIBILITY

Doing what is probable is not a *bad* place to start something. It is, after all, *one* of the possibilities. Trying what has a reasonable chance of success can be just the thing you need to get something going. Once you start to get an outcome or two it may prove easier to become more adventurous. But the adventure is not into some wild and risky unknown. That is not the purpose of the creative world. The point is that when you let go of the limitations of the winner/loser world - that you *must* have a successful result - you cease to be limited to logical and rational ideas. This allows your intuitive creativity to take you in directions that your conscious mind does not control. This is the thrill of possibility over probability.

What you think is possible is limited by what you *think*. More to the point, you are limited to what you think you can think – what you believe. Fortunately, your body doesn't sit and wait for your rational mind to do everything (remember the marvel of feeling hungry).

Sometimes our body will incline us in some direction or other. An example is when dealing with physical activity or sport. How do we really 'know' what sport we will enjoy? Of course, the best way to find out is to play some different things and your body will show you which types of things you are naturally inclined toward. There are lots of children who play the dominant sport of their school or community, but some have a terrible time. This 'terrible time' is just their body showing that it wants other possibilities. It is also wise to be wary of stereotyping physical appearance. If a child is tall then it is often assumed they should play basketball, but if they can't play well, they shouldn't have to suffer for the sake of a stereotype. Maybe they prefer chess. There is always another possibility.

This is the same for intellectual things. Who would have thought that I would want to write, but if you look back at my past, in between the stereotypical 'boy' things I did, I always did like to write. I wrote poems to my girlfriend and liked to be in the school play. The messages were there and I am glad to have listened.

Adventuring into the unlimited realm of possibility has a number of naturally developed safeguards. We are naturally inclined to follow a path that maximises our strengths and talents. The creative world exercises and practices are designed to encourage these natural inclinations. Allow yourself and those around you to discover their own pathway of possibility. Living a probable life is so... predictable.

TRANSACTION / INTERACTION

A simple way to know if you are transacting instead of openly interacting is to imagine you are playing cards. Are you holding some of your cards to your chest? If you are, then you are exhibiting the caution of transaction.

The first thing to consider is whether being cautious is a healthy creative reaction to the behaviour of the other person or the nature of the situation. I am not advocating that you should instantly trust everyone and put all your cards on the table. It may take time to create a lifestyle and a personal environment that is less dependent or dominated by winner/loser world experiences. *You* might feel you are in the creative world, but that doesn't mean that anyone else is.

You will often have to deal with the winner/loser world, but you will be able to interact in the creative world way. It's not easy when some people are living the creative world way and some are not. This is especially true in your home or family. It is important to remind you that the winner/loser world is not going to go away when you enter the creative world, it just ceases to dominate and control your life. That is where so many other programs, systems and beliefs come unstuck. You can't make the winner/loser world disappear by blindly embracing an alternative. Shutting your eyes doesn't make anything disappear. It just puts you in the dark!

Being 'mindful' is a word that I use more and more as I experience the creative world. It takes into account the fragility of our conscious awareness and the difficulty in getting the right message. Being mindful is a result of the *that's interesting* technique. Taking a little time allows us to consider, respond, emotionally appreciate and allow the 'ahh principle' to be noticed. It is not necessary to jump in with an almighty rush or to hold back in a harsh way. There is time for *that's interesting*, there's time for *random inspiration* and other tools. There is always time to be happy as you mindfully consider the possibilities.

ARROGANCE / CONFIDENCE

I remember when Mohammed Ali would parade around declaring, "I am the greatest". It seemed a very arrogant and annoying thing to do. The difficulty was that he *was* the greatest. There was no other athlete like him at that time. So, was he arrogant or just truthful? This puzzled me for many years. Understanding the winner/loser world clarifies it somewhat: he was doing a number of things.

Ali expressed his confidence and determination in himself by responding to his natural talents and following them to their fullest expression. He was also giving his opponents an impossible task. How could you ever defeat 'the greatest'? So, he was using arrogance to dominate his opponent and gain an advantage. The fact that what he was saying was true just made his intimidation that much more powerful and effective.

When someone needs to prove something or tries to drag others down, then that is easily done with a display of arrogance. But it is not always that simple. From the creative world perspective an accusation of arrogance usually warrants a *that's interesting* investigation because sometimes it is not the accused that has a problem, but the accuser. Just because some people feel that they are being shown up or put down doesn't mean that the accused person is doing it. Sometimes it comes from their own negative attitude and they are looking for someone or something to blame for their feelings. Arrogance is the winner/loser way of gaining an advantage. In the creative world it is only interesting.

♦♦♦ DEALING WITH THE DEMONS ♦♦♦

In writing this book I was able to look at my past… the harshness of my childhood so that … they became part of my strength, part of my motivation.

Li Cunxin, author *Mao's Last Dancer*

RIGHT AND WRONG

The best words to use to stop a *right and wrong* argument are, 'I don't mind'. This is very different from "I don't care" which is a big winner/loser world whinge. The worst thing to say is "whatever you say", which is a wasted capitulation hoping that you can elicit some guilt. Start with "that's interesting" and consider the issue from the perspective that you truly don't mind who is right. What will happen then is that the thing that is being argued about becomes information and that information can lead to the creation of an entirely new outcome. From a stupid 'right or wrong' battle can emerge a new and exciting possibility.

GOOD AND BAD

Take some time when results seem good or bad to allow yourself the opportunity to properly consider the situation. Everything can have a silver lining, not because you must have a positive attitude or because there must be some reason for things or because of any attitude that may cause you to 'look through rose coloured glasses'. Everything has a silver lining because the creative process never stops. Every outcome, even those that are undesirable, is the stepping-stone to a new outcome. Everything has a silver lining because it *does*!

When someone feels a loser, there is no point just defying logic and saying the opposite. When a child comes last in their class, there's no point saying that they really *are* clever and they will be able to come first one day. These are all attempts to say, "You are not a loser, you are a winner!" This just traps everyone more in the winner/loser world. The positive, creative way is to ask the question, "What can we create with that?" There are so many questions that might arise from your child coming bottom of the class: What is the teacher like? Who do they sit next to? What subjects are they good at? How does someone get a good mark? Etc.

Ask, enquire, learn and be fascinated by everything because anything might be the catalyst for the creation of something amazing.

EXPECTATION

It is natural to have some degree of expectation. The ability to anticipate and project ourselves into the future is a wonderful human ability. Expectation as a demon, however, is when your future projection is clouded by the necessity to produce a winning result. The winner/loser world puts a very unhealthy pressure on us to *know* what the future will bring.

Prediction has become a very popular skill and is sought out on many levels. Stock market predictions are keenly sought after and highly paid for. We expect that a doctor will give a 'clean bill of health' not just for today, but for a period to come. Quite a lot of counselling is done in relation to career and future direction. This can help people set a course of direction for their lives. Religious prediction of the nature of life after death can be a principle foundation of behaviour for some. Of course, psychic prediction has been utilised for millennia. I think there are some very interesting and useful elements in the practice of psychic prediction. My concern with any prediction system is that the client is seeking to gain some advantage in order not to be a loser, in order to follow a successful line. Frankly, they want some guarantee of a good result because the stress of not knowing is too hard to bear. This can so easily lead to disappointment.

The trick when you imagine into the future is to have an idea of the direction you wish to go, but still allow the process of creative interaction to produce outcomes that may not have been expected. Sometimes these outcomes may completely change your direction to a much better course.

FAULT AND BLAME

This one is quite simple to deal with – just stop it. The only information that is important is what we learn. The only important thing to *do* is to discover what can be created. Certainly, it is difficult when the winner/loser world spoils any positive effort by putting people on the defensive, but it is important to resist.

Sometimes clients tell me it is not their fault because they have told the other person not to do it. Just telling someone is like handing over responsibility. Helping someone to learn is more than that. I have been asked how often you should try to teach someone something. The answer is obvious: until they have learnt. When the problem is that people don't listen or understand, then there is a clear message to look at why they don't hear or understand. There could be language problems, attitude differences, responsibility issues and more.

ISOLATION

The sense of loneliness that comes from isolation may vary in intensity, but it is unmistakable. It can happen in so many ways: when you feel like you can't talk to people, especially the ones you love; when you feel that you have to do everything yourself; when you are convinced that nobody cares about you; when you find that you don't care about anyone; when it is easier to ignore people than to say hello; when you feel as though the governments of the world are out of your control; when you are overlooked in your workplace; when you have a great piece of news, but no-one to tell it to; or when you can't even see yourself in the mirror with any pride. These are the types of experiences that drive us into isolation. As I wrote earlier, how can so many people be lonely when there are so many of us?

The simple answer to isolation is to connect and interact. Anything creative is a great start. People tend to forget the winner/loser world when they are involved in creative things. This is where outward creative expression can be a useful trigger to open the door to the creative world. There are a host of creative classes and groups that could interest your personal talents. You can find information at your local council, church or school. There are writers groups, art classes, acting, singing, chess, local history, garden groups, charitable work and even toastmaster public speaking. One of the simplest creative acts is to smile. Spend time with people and enjoy their company. The pathway to the creative world is not constrained by any skill or personal quality. Everyone can smile, at least for a moment and, with a bit of practice, even most of the time.

GUILT

This is the one that gets you time and time again. The big word in the *guilt world* is 'should'. I *should* have done this; you *should* have done that; things *should* be this way and all the other 'shoulds'. An amusing friend used to wryly say, "Don't should on yourself!" The other key word of guilt is responsibility. This, of course, incorporates the *fault and blame* demon and can lead us into all kinds of trouble and discomfort. The word, responsibility, has been totally lost into a winner/loser world definition. It's a bit complex to explain in a paragraph or two, so I have expanded on it in Section 2.

The basic cure to guilt is *that's interesting* and also *tell me everything in your head*. Quite often people try to invoke guilt as a defence against their own guilt. In the winner/loser world it is a common practice to try and make people feel or look worse. This doesn't make them a winner, but they feel they are less of a loser.

There is absolutely no winning with guilt. There is no winning with any of the demons. It seems that there is no winning in the winner/loser world. Not for an extended time at any rate. In a world that peddles the value of instant gratification it may be possible to be satisfied with a series of minor and temporary wins. It doesn't make me feel happy and I have yet to find anyone for whom it does.

◆◆◆◆◆◆◆◆◆◆◆

That concludes the first part of the book. You should now have enough information and practical tools to help you integrate the creative world way in to your life. You should also have a clear grasp of the winner/loser world and how it has maintained such a grasp over us. I hope you have already changed irreversibly.

Now that Section 1 has satisfied our immediate needs for definition and explanation, I would like to move on to ideas and thoughts about life from the creative world perspective. Section 2 is intended to take you further down the path of thinking and understanding, of being interested and inspired. Now that we have completed the hard task of explanation and establishing a new vocabulary, we should see what we can create.

When Alice went through the looking glass, everything was changed, and seemed to be back-to-front. That is how the creative world might seem to you at first. Section 2 is, therefore, called 'Through the Looking Glass'.

But firstly, the first Parable.

● THE PARABLE OF THE BEEF ROAST ●

Young Mary was a very inquisitive five-year-old, but also quite thoughtful. She would watch something being done and then, after a time, she would ask a question. Quite often the question showed just how observant she was. Her Mum would always encourage Mary to ask.

One day Mary's mum was preparing a roast dinner. Her brother had to peel potatoes, which Mary thought was a good thing. Her mum prepared the meat with a few select spices and finished by rubbing the top of the meat with salt. Mary was just about to ask about the salt when her mum picked up the sharp knife and cut a slice of meat off the end. This made the meat a bit more like a square, but Mary had to ask.

"Why did you cut that bit off the end of the meat, Mummy?" she asked, tilting her head and slightly squinting to show that she really wanted to know. Her mum stopped what she was doing for a moment. Mary saw that her mum's eyebrows moved inward making a wrinkle in the skin between them and her head tilted a bit, too. After a few moments her mum replied, "I don't really know. My mum, your grandma, taught me. I guess you had better ask her when she comes for dinner tonight."

Mary was usually quite patient, but by the time Grandma arrived she was nearly bursting with curiosity. Grandma was barely in the door before she began her question. "Grandma, Grandma! You know when you make a roast like Mummy's doing tonight and you do all that stuff and rub it in and get a boy to peel the potatoes and make beans even though I don't really like them…" Mary was almost out of breath. Her grandmother patted her gently on the head and smoothed her curls, "Slow down little one. Let me get inside and you can tell me all about it."

Mary had to wait until her grandmother had said hello to everyone else, put down all her packages and finally settled into the comfortable armchair that she always sat in before she could start again. "Grandma, why did Mummy cut off the little bit of meat on the end?" "Good heavens!" replied her grandmother, "Is that what all this fuss is about? Well, let me see." Mary watched as her grandmother's eyebrows moved inward and she made the same wrinkles, only bigger and more of them. "I have to confess, young miss, I don't know. I was taught by my mother, your great-grandmother. You're going to have to ask her."

Now, Mary was a quiet and patient girl, but that was because parents were supposed to know what they were doing and answer her questions when she asked, not send her reeling down the list of all the relatives she had. Still, she had a new task. She had to get her mum to take her on a visit to Grammsy in the hospital.

Things take time in the world of adults, much more time than satisfies a child who has a question. Mary thought she was going to go stark raving mad (she heard that on an old film on television and would use it when referring to her brother). Finally the day came and Mary was off to solve the puzzle.

As they walked up the path Mary was reminded that you had to be quiet and not do things too quickly with Grammsy. When they got inside she sat on a chair very quietly until they had rearranged Grammsy's pillows and given her a little drink. All the adults gave her a hug and a kiss and Mary sat quietly. Eventually, Grammsy looked over to Mary and a big smile spread across her face. "Good heavens! Who is this sitting so quietly on the chair? Mary, I haven't seen you in a long time. Look how you've grown." Her great-grandmother put out her hand and beckoned with a slight nod of her head. "Come here and let me see you a bit closer." Mary loved her Grammsy very much, but the hospital was a bit scary. The beds were made of metal, there were bottles and tubes and strange little machines that looked like little televisions, but there was never any television shows on. Still, she walked carefully over and took her great-grandmothers hand. "Now, what have you been doing?" asked Grammsy.

Mary thought she had better get right to it. She'd seen her Grammsy fall asleep quite suddenly once before and she couldn't risk it, so she got straight to the point. "Grammsy, you know how you taught Grandma how to cook a roast?"

"Yes, sweetie, I did indeed."

"And, then Grandma taught my Mummy how to cook a roast?"

"Well, I should think so. No one cooks a roast like your Grammsy. Did she make sure that one of the boys peeled the potatoes?"

"Yes, my brother did that, but then before Mummy put the meat in the pan she cut a piece off the end and no one seems to know why. You're my last great-grandma. Do you know?"

"Well, let me see." Grammsy's eyebrows began to head together and make those wrinkles. Mary was horrified, but then the eyebrows stopped moving inward and they started moving outwards and upward. Then Grammsy's eyes opened very wide and she began to laugh. By this time all the women were fixed on Grammsy and what she would say. "Well, Mary, I'll tell you. I cut that little piece of meat off the end because in my kitchen, when I was cooking roast dinners, my roasting pan was too small. That's all!"

Three generations of women were dumbfounded. Mary looked at her mother and her grandmother and for the first time realised that adults don't necessarily know everything. From that day on, to the annoyance of many a person, Mary was happy to learn the right way to do things, but you had better know why or she would be asking questions.

◆ ◆ ◆ ◆ ◆ ◆ ◆ ◆ ◆ ◆ ◆

The moral of the story? Rules may guarantee you will achieve the goal, but questions can expose whether the goals are worth achieving. What possibilities lie unimagined behind the screen of unconsidered rules?

SECTION 2

<u>THROUGH THE LOOKING GLASS</u>

<u>CONTENTS</u>

♦♦♦ INTRODUCTION ♦♦♦

It is wonderful to have a great idea or an inspiring realisation. It is only natural to want to share it. We are a very creative species and ideas are erupting all the time. Very often, however, a creative, inspired idea is not always accurate and is often imperfect. Imagination and inspiration give us the moment of creation, not the evolved universe. An idea needs to be examined to find out what it is about.

Einstein was a great supporter of imagination. He is quoted as saying, *"Imagination is more important than knowledge. Knowledge is limited. Imagination encircles the world".* He is said to have imagined what it would be like to run beside a beam of light to give him insights into his theory of light particles. This imaginative beginning set up the process of arduous work that was eventually presented in 1905. Together with his other papers on gravity and relativity, Einstein changed the world of science and human progress. His imaginative ideas and thoughtful considerations produced the knowledge that has been breeding more ideas ever since.

I have heard some wonderful ideas over the years and some very inspiring thoughts: go with the flow; trust the universe to provide; keep an open mind; love conquers all; universal consciousness; and universal mind. I find these ideas very inspiring, but I have never really heard a good explanation or discussion about the foundations of these ideas. Sometimes the explanation is in a circle with itself: you will understand about going with the flow when you go with the flow. Even the great mythologist, Joseph Campbell, who propagated the mantra 'follow your bliss' never really made it clear for me just what that entailed. Now, however, we know so much more about the brain and the mind that it is possible to give these heartfelt inspirations greater foundation. To put it simply, we can make more sense of them.

In Section 2 we will look at the foundation stones of knowledge that support the ideas, questions and theories of the 'winner/loser world' and the 'winner/loser world problem'. This section also looks at the way the creative view of the world can change our perception and our beliefs. We need to be clear on whether things *do* change when you live in the creative world and also whether they change for the better.

Section 2 celebrates the magic of thought that comes from the miracle of inspiration. At the beginning of each chapter I have included the thought, question or idea that inspired the writing. What thoughts come to your mind as you read? What inspirations? Please share these with others, or with me if you wish. Come to the website, start or join a blog, write a letter to the editor, just don't hold anything in. Interact and allow the extraordinary process of creativity to produce outcomes. Every outcome will change the world, even if just a little bit. That is what the creative world is all about.

◆◆ IS THE WINNER/LOSER WORLD NATURAL? ◆◆

> THOUGHT: *It would be easier to understand and accept the winner/loser world if it had some foundation in natural human behaviour.*

That *we* have actually created the winner/loser world is quite ironic, but it is exactly what you might expect when you understand the way the 7 Demons affect you. We have allowed this competitive, win at all costs, disengaged winner/loser world to dominate our lives and send many of us down a pathway of emotional dysfunction. This may seem like a fairly stupid thing for a species to do, but we are still evolving. What we know now is that even though the body may change quite slowly, our thoughts can change within hours, days and certainly weeks. New understanding and life changes are only a 'mind-beat' away.

I suggest that the winner/loser world was created on the shoulders of our instinct for survival. In situations of life and death it is vital to win: you win - you live; you lose - you die. This instinct exists in many species so we must have also evolved something else. We did. Somewhere in the last 150,000 years or so, humans developed a mind. This was an amazing step because it allowed us to plan and imagine. It has allowed us to share thoughts and ideas and even more incredibly, has enabled us to gather together and co-operate to achieve greater things than is possible by an individual. This has helped make us the dominant species on the planet.

We can imagine thoughts about the future. This allows us to plan and prepare, which is an enormous benefit to us as a species. An unfortunate side effect of this is that we don't have very good control over the sorts of things we can imagine. Amongst all the glorious things we can see in our mind's eye we can also imagine horrible things. We have been able to invent the concept of fate, knowledge of the inevitability of death and the possibility of future failure. This change in our brain and mind gives us the capacity to *believe* we might be in danger even when we are not. It has allowed us to shift our focus from the possibilities of what we can create in the present, to the probabilities of what we might do in the future and what that future should be. John Lennon put it well when he wrote, 'Life is what happens to you while you're busy making other plans'. Mostly the plans we are making are plans to be a winner.

Because we have decided that winning is a measure of success, we have taught ourselves to *believe* that winners are the successful people. Equally, if you are not a winner, then you are not a success. The other thing we have predetermined is that if you are not a success you will have difficulty in the world, because the winner/loser world only rewards success. Even more so, if you are a loser you may not be able to successfully function in the world at all and risk having an awful life. This has led us to connect the idea of social failure to our chance of surviving and this thought can trigger our instinct for survival. This happens because our body has not yet evolved to deal with issues of tomorrow's failure, only an immediate threat. Our thoughts that breed fears about things that aren't even happening to us yet are simply interpreted by our body as danger, imminent attack and a threat to survival. So, that is the way we react.

When you encounter, or believe that a situation is vital to your survival, your natural instincts kick in. Your body puts into action the instinct of fight-flight-or-freeze (sympathetic nervous system). Because we don't know how to tell the difference between a real life-and-death struggle and one that is only imagined, our body continues to react to the threat. Because the imagined threats of the winner/loser world don't go away, our body assumes a chronic, long-term state of fear and distress.

In addition to this, when the winner/loser world makes us think we are failures, our instinctive systems respond and our body focuses on short-term survival. These take precedence over other, less urgent systems. Survival is the most important thing. We shut down our digestive system, we shut down the sleep system, we activate the intensity of our muscles, we reduce the sensitivity of our skin and extremities, and we disengage from community interaction to focus on resisting and repelling the threat.

The question now is: Why do we *believe* that non-life threatening concerns, such as how much money you make, whether you are too fat or who is right about politics, are issues of life and death? This, amongst other things, has a lot to do with the nature of society.

In short, a group of people will develop a set of organising agreements to make communal life reasonably functional. As groups grow in size it becomes more difficult to maintain the agreements because it is impossible to be mentally aware of all the needs of too large a group (anthropologist, Robin Dunbar, suggests that a workable number is around 150 people). To solve this problem, social understandings and agreements were institutionalised into set structures and systems. These structures and systems become relatively rigid and so when new people enter society it seems easier for the new people to adjust, rather than the whole society. We begin to be measured by our ability to satisfy and fit in with those structures and systems. These many and various social structures and systems become the foundation of our way of life and the foundation of our value as a person.

The truth of it is that society is not designed for any individual, but only as a general system to manage a population. This means that the social system is often at great odds with your personal needs, capabilities and natural inclinations. In fact, it is *most likely* to be at odds with everyone to some degree.

There is a wise, anonymous saying that all you need in life is food in your belly, a roof over your head and the freedom to do what you want (and these must be achieved in that order). In the 'real world', providing a roof over your head can involves a surprising amount of effort: taxes, council rates, insurance, maintenance, a house that shows your social wealth and worth, gardens, cable connections and so on and so on. Food becomes dependent on supermarkets, marketing and diet fads. By the time you get around to doing what you want it has become an almost impossible task because you are too busy or too tired or too stressed or you've simply forgotten what it is that you want anyway.

In the end, these unnecessary complexities, these *things,* become the measure of your success. This becomes entwined with your instinctive capacity to survive and successfully reproduce. It is not long before we have convinced our body that the more *things* we have the better are our chances to survive and reproduce. Therefore, the more socially important you are the more likely you are to get the opportunities to get the things that will ensure your survival. Suddenly you are stuck in a loop of activity that shifts ordinary social activities into measures of your social worth and social importance and, therefore, your capacity to survive. It seems funny when someone says, "I'll just *die* if I can't get one of those things", but many a thing is said in jest. The sad thing is that this is what is *actually* happening to many people. They forfeit their lives because they can't get the *things*. Some forfeit their lives because they *have* got the things, but they have no happiness. The 'real world' is getting us at both ends. The great neuroscientist Robert Sapolsky puts it simply by saying that we are designed "for the danger of an immediate attack, not a thirty year mortgage".

If our mind continues to worry or imagine negatively, creating fearful feelings, then our body tries to cope with fight-or-flight. It is, however, like some biological catch-22 because there is no need to fight or fly. What the body does instead is become 'tight-and-ready'. Being 'tight and ready' for a prolonged period is something very new to human beings. It is a sort of 'just-in-case' mode, which is a completely unnatural state of being. The tight-and-ready mode is a state of prolonged stress. Prolonged stress (among many things) leads to anxiety and anxiety leads to depression. By depression, I mean a chemical change in the neural system that changes our capacity to successfully deal with our environment. It is ironic that the winner/loser world struggle for success in order to improve our chance of survival is what is killing us, or at the very least, driving us crazy.

This long-term state of stress is what disturbs our emotional wellbeing. Even though the 'real world' gives us no escape from the pressure of winning, we are so used to it now that we don't even see these day-to-day concerns as winner/loser issues. But they are: Do I have enough money? Am I pretty enough? Is that person making fun of me? Will I pass my exam? What if I don't come first in my class? Have I got a beautiful partner? Do they like me? Are the children going to get good jobs? Which ice cream will I choose? Am I doing the right thing? What if I am wrong? Why does everyone think it was my fault? Why do I think it was my fault? Why don't people just do as I say? The body tenses, our emotions fray, we become concerned and cautious and even distrustful, we can't think straight and our mind shuts down from learning and it becomes almost impossible to successfully interact with others because of our pre-occupation with ourselves. We are dominated by the pervading fear of not winning - of being a loser.

A much more successful and natural response to personal difficulty is to connect with the people around us, to find solace, comfort and advice from others. This can include family, friends and other members of the 'tribe'. We are designed to overcome individual difficulty with communal help and support. But the winner/loser struggle is based on individual success, which resists enlisting help and support. This creates the 'winner/loser problem' where connection is vital for emotional health, but separation is necessary for social success.

So, can we say that because the winner/loser world has emerged from natural behaviour then it must be okay? It is without doubt that your survival instinct will save your life more than once and possibly someone else's life, too, but it will not help you become a better person. It will not help you forge stronger relationships or lead to a happier life. Quite the opposite. That is why we have developed the *equally* vital instinct of community and interaction. One instinct saves us from the attack by a sabre-toothed tiger and the other gives us companions with whom we can tell the story and embrace with love. You simply cannot embrace when separated. The winner/loser world might well be sending the human race into extinction as we kill ourselves trying to survive - to win.

♦♦♦ SOCIETY ♦♦♦

THOUGHT: *Where does a society come from?*

Society is an interesting thing because, in the ideal, it doesn't really exist. Not as a *thing* anyway. It is not something you can see or touch. It is a concept: society and culture form out of the nature and the needs of the people within it; it is an outcome of complex interactions; and it is a system that arises to help people live together.

Society is an averaging or a composite of the needs, ideas, values and behaviours of the people. A society is not about one person. If one person changes it is rare for a society to change. There seems to be a critical mass of population that *can* motivate change, although this mass can vary. So, society is a natural outcome of the existence of a population and it is an expression of the broadly acceptable beliefs of that population; it can change, but tends not to, yet it endeavours to be relevant to the population despite the nature of the population changing faster than society's ability to express that nature.

Society deals in general needs and stereotypes because it is a design for the larger group, not an individual. A social stereotype, therefore, cannot be an *aspiration* of an individual because it is only a generalised *expression* of the population. Equally, society should not be an encompassing 'world'. But that's the way it seems. How does a social system become a 'real world'?

The infrastructure that the population *builds* around the tenets of their society turns society into a thing, an entity: the buildings; the economic systems; the rituals and practices; the common beliefs; the institutions and organizations; and all the other sub-groups, make a society a tangible thing. These structures are comparatively rigid and become the accepted 'norm'. Once they are established, they are difficult to change or adjust and even if there is change, it is slow. This 'norm' becomes a benchmark and a measure of an individual's worth or value. Under these conditions, it not only makes sense, but is essential for an individual to want to fit into the social structure and meet society's expectations. It is by satisfying society's expectations that many people are considered, and consider themselves to be, successful.

It is unfortunate that a society is rarely an expression of the greater qualities of any particular individual. It is also not the function of a society to be an expression of unusual values. Its simple purpose is to provide a mechanism that allows the people within it to function together. A society need do no more than that. By definition, no one can truly satisfy any of society's stereotypes, either individually or broadly, because these stereotypes do not truly exist. For many the difficulty of trying to conform becomes emotionally disturbing. For some it is just impossible

So, if society has become a world unto itself, is it reasonable to think that our society is a 'winner/loser world'? Perhaps not in every way, but the winner/loser way is clearly the dominating force.

How does this work? We live in a competitive, success and achievement-oriented society. The desired outcome to any situation is to win. To be a loser is a terrible thing. In order to be a winner you must know what winning is - you must know what 'the winning thing' is. If you know what makes a 'winner' then you know what to aim for. This is where the structures of society take over from the individual. Social standards become the determinant of what is considered 'winning'. What you as an individual may think, feel or believe is almost irrelevant at any given time. Your thoughts, feelings and beliefs require a great deal of effort and time before they can create social change. Alain de Botton wrote an excellent description of society as an expression of the winner/loser world in his book *Status Anxiety*. He makes some valuable suggestions of how to deal with this anxiety, but I feel that these are effective band-aids rather than cures.

In *Choose Hope* I described society as a 'wonderful playground, but a terrible master'. I think it's reasonable to assume that you can interpret much of society and its structures as being a dominantly winner/loser system. The goal is to come out on top, be successful, have more, etc. You can easily describe successful social behaviour in the terms of the 7 Demons: people want to be right and good; not be at fault or to blame when things go wrong; be just that bit better than everyone else; receive praise; and not only avoid guilt, but make sure that other people (especially competitors) are held back by guilt and responsibility.

Society can be seen as a form of parent in that it provides care, sets up expectations, directs moral values, provides opportunity for your personal expression and defines the boundaries of that expression. In psychological theory our relationship with parents and its effect on us is called *attachment theory* .We develop attachments in our lives in direct relation to the quality of our relationship with our parents (as well as other strong influences in our experience). This affects how we construct our sense of self and how we build our ongoing emotional wellbeing.

It is important for well-balanced development for a parent to act with 'contingency'. This simply means that the parent responds in a caring and attendant way that clearly reflects our needs. They do this by showing that there is understanding and acceptance which produces a positive response. All this allows you to feel connected to someone other than yourself and allows you to develop a strong sense of self (for deeper reference I suggest reading Daniel Siegel's books *The Developing Mind* and *Parenting from the Inside Out*). For example, when a child expresses that they are hungry they feel a natural sense of safety when the parent listens, responds and attends to that need. The outcome may not even be that the child is given food, but a connected and interactive response occurs that is contingent with the child's needs. This is not about children being given anything they want, but about providing a clear sense of engaged relationship.

Contingent interaction will mostly produce what is called a secure attachment, which allows for a positive and helpful development of the self. The bottom line is that we establish a balanced sense of ourselves in a balanced and attentive environment. Society, however, becomes like a super-parent which is only satisfied with achievement that is measured by its own predetermined expectations. These expectations commonly have little or no direct regard for our personal wants and desires, so we can feel the absence of contingent attention and, therefore, develop an insecure sense of attachment. This affects and diminishes our positive sense of self as we grow from puberty into adulthood. When we look back at our human parents they often seem complicit in the whole thing as they encourage us, reward us and chide us based on our ability to live up to social needs and expectations. Throughout our lives we may rebel against our parents, rarely thinking that the problem is our parent's parent – society.

It is no wonder that alternative sub-societies are so inviting. These provide a separate place, a sort of refuge, where an individual can feel more loved, included, cared for and nurtured. When you are in a group small enough (usually less than 150) or you share a belief that presents a perfect, contingent parent or you are simply far enough away from the 'madding crowd', you can feel as though you have escaped, found solace and been restored. But to my mind, escape is not an answer. It may be an alternative or a refuge, which may be helpful in the short term, but it's not an answer. The best answer is knowledge and wisdom. That can only come from questions, curiosity and contemplation. And it comes from what you create from those questions, discoveries and contemplations – this is the creative world way.

◆◆◆ THE BARRIER BETWEEN THE ◆◆◆
WINNER/LOSER WORLD AND THE
CREATIVE WORLD

THOUGHT: *The first reaction to something new and challenging is, surprisingly often, hesitation or even rejection. Why do we do that?*

What makes it so difficult to embrace the creative world way? Or, at least, what makes it so difficult to stop behaving and thinking in the winner/loser world way? These questions bring us back to basic human behaviour, habits and the creation of new connections in the brain.

Essentially it is an issue of the devil you know versus the devil you don't on one hand, and the devil you know versus the alternative that requires too much effort on the other. The winner/loser world's demons affect our better judgement on both counts. The winner/loser world is so entrenched in our infrastructure, political and social systems and day-to-day experiences that it is easy to assume that a change might be a risk, that something may be lost. It's like a child who won't taste something new because they fear what they don't know and feel safer in what they do know. This creates a life of rigidity and boredom. Many seem to prefer boredom than risking an idea like the creative world, even if it promises wonderful things. The fear of being wrong or being at fault can strangle the whole process of adopting the creative world way of living.

The second issue is the difficulty involved in learning something new. The old saying goes, 'you can't teach old dogs new tricks'. I don't know about old dogs, but I know that that is not true of human beings. Brain research, especially in recent years, has shown, beyond any doubt, that the brain is able to grow new synapses and neurons at any age. We can expand and adapt our brain at any time – if we want to. There is, of course, a process.

It's not magic. New brain cells don't just snap into existence, but it doesn't take long if you are persistent and determined.

Through the insightful research of neuroscientists like Dr Ernest Rossi we know that new synapses that create new pathways in the brain begin to take shape in about 90 minutes. This means that new ideas and new realisations begin to take form after just an hour or so of focus. You may have noticed that you need a break when learning new things after about 90 minutes. Films tend to be about 90-120 minutes long. We often give high praise to a film that goes for three hours if it can maintain our interest! These new thought pathways in your brain then need about 30 days of reinforcing to form very strong pathways and overrule the old ways of thinking. You may have noticed that when you start a new job or a new sport it takes a couple of weeks to feel like you're getting it, but after a month or so it's easy. You may even feel like a bit of an idiot for finding it so difficult in the first place. When it starts to feels like second nature that means that you have created and reinforced a new neural pathway. You have learnt a new trick.

The winner/loser world holds people back from learning because within those few weeks you can look like a stupid loser as you struggle to learn. It is interesting that businesses will often give people 'trainee' badges to help customers understand that someone is just learning. This is a very creative idea, but when you are in the winner/loser world wearing a badge that says you don't know what you're doing only amplifies the fact that you are inept. Some of the more enlightened companies have training sessions that change after about 90 minutes. Training continues with assistance for about two weeks. After a month people are expected to manage on their own. That is, basically, how the brain prefers to work.

You should bear this in mind as you learn to move away from the winner/loser world ways and take on the creative world ways. This book may be a 'red pill', but it is not a 'magic bullet' or an 'instant answer'. Broadly, instant changes are not genuine, although sometimes it may feel like that. When you finally have an 'ahh' moment it may feel sudden, but it is usually after a lot of non-conscious processing. The penny may drop, but it has probably been waiting at the top of the slot for some time.

That is what the 6 Practices are all about. If you use these practices regularly it will soon become second nature. When you use *that's interesting* as a regular practice, you will find that you give yourself the opportunity to pause and contemplate your actions and, at the same time, remind yourself just how interesting life really is. Some people who have been working with the 6 Practices have found that they find themselves saying or thinking *that's interesting* so often that it feels like they are doing it all the time. After a few days, however, and certainly after a couple of weeks, they began to reduce the amount of times they would say it out loud. It becomes a part of the normal day-to-day way of doing things. It is wonderful to find interesting things in everything. And why not?

The same thing goes for *what can I create with this*, but it doesn't take long before you are creating something without having to think about it. That is because you have a strong, reinforced neural pathway that comes into play whenever you interact. It is such a wonderful, liberating feeling.

So, the barrier is mostly about our inertia, our fear of change and our unrealistic demand that good things should happen instantaneously. Many of the benefits of living the creative world way may be *felt* instantaneously, but they still take time to form in your brain and become a part of your mind. Don't let the winner/loser world trap you in its rigid grasp. Even if things seem a bit chaotic at first, don't worry, that is often just a knee-jerk reaction to the realisation that your freedom has been so constrained for so long. As you settle into the creative experience you will find harmony and even more to the point, harmony will find you.

♦♦♦ RESPONSE-ABILITY ♦♦♦

THOUGHT: *It is not so much that I react to things, but that I definitely will react to things. Reaction seems an unavoidable aspect of living.*

To be able to respond to the world around you is a natural disposition. We are hard-wired to act responsively. There are a number of ways in which we do this. We use a set of senses that record and respond to stimuli: sight, hearing, taste, touch and smell. We also have more abstract senses that respond to the world around us and within us: emotions, thoughts, attitudes and empathy. All these senses participate in 'responding'. Yet, we are even more complex. All these senses can be responding on different levels of consciousness and attention.

We have instincts. Instincts protect us by activating a response without having to think. These are built into our system. We retract from something painful. Our instinct of fight-flight-freeze comes into play when we are surprised or frightened by something. We have instincts that regulate breathing and heartbeat. We have an instinct to play and socialize.

We also have urges, which are not as irresistible as instincts, but are built into our system. These are seen in sexual urges, selfish urges, aggressive urges, an urge to win and others that are established in the older areas of our brain. Some of these urges are what we call 'animal urges', but they are also called 'uninhibited urges'. It is possible, however, to develop thinking processes that over-ride or inhibit some instincts and urges. We are born with only about half our mature brain. Much of the brain growth in children is in the neo-cortex. You might say that we are born with our 'animal brain' and we grow the 'thinking brain' as we go. As we begin to think about things and learn about our world we develop inhibitions to our primal urges and in doing so are able to form civilized societies. That's the principle, anyway.

As you become more aware of the world and what it means it becomes a less scary place. The degree to which something frightens you is directly related to the speed in which you work it out. This means that you may instinctively freeze at a strange sound, but the fear can be 'extinguished' quite quickly when you realize that it is just the cat. Life experiences become very complex, especially when other people are involved, and so 'figuring something out' can take up a lot of brainpower. Even still, what you think about the world and how you think about the world has a direct bearing on how much it scares you. The capacity to think about the world successfully is often called our 'common sense' or our 'reasoning'. Another description is to 'act maturely' or to 'act your age'.

Just to complicate things further, it is also possible to develop thoughts during life that have a similar affect us as our non-conscious urges. These thoughts involve our inner response to and memory of trauma and shock. This is evident in things like post-traumatic stress disorder, phobias and distrust, like the fear of affection after a relationship ends painfully. Lastly, we even have a set of thought programs that can over-ride common sense, maturity and sometimes even self-protection. These fall into the category of beliefs. Beliefs affect the way the world appears to us and is often described as our 'perspective' or 'point of view'.

That is quite a list of response mechanisms that affect our responses. A number seem to be out of our direct control, but when we respond to the stimuli of the world around us, all these elements come into play. No wonder we sometimes feel like we don't know how to react. However, with all these possible ways of responding, we must have developed a natural system to moderate and allow these different systems to work together. If we had a chaotic mess every time there was a stimulus to respond to, then our species would not have survived.

The natural mechanism we use to make sense of our responses is a combination of our ability to learn and our ability to be aware of how we feel. By noticing when we feel good (because we are creating desirable outcomes) we are able to know what is beneficial to learn. We can do the same when we have undesirable outcomes, although we learn what we *don't* want to do again so that we modify it next time. This is the natural path of the creative world way: use what you have in this moment and learn something beneficial to take into the next moment. The winner/loser world, on the other hand, leaves us with a disastrous confusion: at the same moment our survival instincts feel there is a threat, but our belief 'urges' are telling us that we will be okay as long as we win.

In the creative world way, not only are we are able to apply what we have learnt to the same type of experience, but also to other experiences. We can relate what we have learnt on a *conceptual* basis. If we didn't do that we would have to learn how to respond to each experience individually. We would need a brain the size of a beach ball just to remember every possibility. Because we don't have a brain the size of a beach ball, knowing what to do in a new situation is often a problem in the winner/loser world. When you have a bad result you often go back to the drawing board because you have failed. If you succeed, however, you are inclined to repeat the same process again in order to maximize your success. This either leads to a boring existence or one that is constantly frustrated because nothing is going the way it 'should' i.e. like it did last time. Putting it more simply, nothing was learnt and so there is no ability to respond creatively.

To open up to interaction in the creative world does not mean to just blindly let go and allow absolutely anything to happen. The idea that you can sit back and let the universe provide doesn't make any sense. It is vital that you are participating in the experience so that you are a part of the outcome. The central tenet of the creative world is that all the information and elements in the situation are included in the process. The central and most common element is always *you*.

Our *response-ability* is learnt over time and through experience. We learn by noticing the way we feel when we respond to things. We learn that we have beliefs and thoughts that are hurting us because we feel stressed and disconnected. We learn when we lash out at the wrong time that we need to pause and consider. We learn lots of things and we become better able to respond in a loving way – in a creative way.

For those of you who have investigated Buddhism, you may recognize similarities here to the concept of mindfulness. I would like to think that these are mutually inclusive ideas.

Mindfulness, in the Buddhist tradition, means that you develop your capacity to appreciate and involve yourself in all of the qualities of your current experience without the interruption or the disturbance of judgment from the past or expectation of the future. Our mind is able to remember the existence of the past and is able to imagine the possibility of the future, but, in reality, the past and the future do not exist. They do exist in the possibilities of our experience, but only as flavours of the current moment. It is only the current moment that we can create with. What we create is taken with us into the future, but when we get there it has become the present. And so it goes on, in each moment.

In Buddhism, this is done through meditation and persistent practice to learn how to focus the mind on an awareness of the present. This practice is also being employed in many aspects of psychotherapy. Dr Daniel Siegel incorporates this process in a very practical way. His work on *Mindsight* is an absolute delight if you wish to look at this further. It is a very interesting teaching and I recommend that you make some investigation of it yourself.

The Buddhist practice follows a very deliberate and practical method to enhance response-ability. This may be more than most of us wish to pursue. I think that we can awaken our ability to respond to our experience more easily and with similar effect. The key is not so much the discipline of the mind (although that is an essential element), but releasing the limitations we place on what is worth noticing and therefore worth responding to. The key is to listen to your body and your feelings. Apply the 6 Practices, especially *what can I create?* and *the problem is a message*. The most important thing to remember is that all and any of your behaviours can be changed, improved or enhanced with a little bit of effort and persistence. You are never 'stuck' with what you do or a hapless 'victim' of the chaos in the world around you. You simply do the best you can and your body will clearly tell you when it is happy and when it is not. Just listen and notice.

♦♦♦ HARMONY ♦♦♦

THOUGHT: *When elements interact they seek to integrate toward a state of harmony.*

That sounds quite good, but is it true? Is it even pointing in the right direction?

In Hollywood there is a banner more than four stories high that reads, "On the day when we can fully trust each other there will be peace on Earth – L Ron Hubbard". Sounds great and makes you feel good for a moment, until you realise that if peace can only come when we are all able to trust each other permanently, then we are looking at a gloomy future. For a start, our ability to understand what we say to each other is full of frailties. It is not wise to fully trust any communication thoughtlessly because language is always less than perfect in conveying meaning.

So, what about my bold thought? Are we really inclined toward a state of harmony? What is a state of harmony? When things interact, do they integrate? Let's look at this statement and see if it is true and helpful. If it is, then this statement provides a solid foundation for the existence of the creative world. If we can be confident that when we interact with others there is a natural inclination toward a harmonious outcome, then the creative world way will definitely be a satisfying experience.

The origins of harmony come from the Latin *harmonia* meaning 'joining' or 'concord' and from Greek *harmos* 'joint'. Webster's Dictionary states: *The just adaptation of parts to each other, in any system or combination of things, or in things, or things intended to form a connected whole.*

The important words here are *connected whole*. This is where independent elements combine to produce something more. Something new has been created, something more than what existed before. This could be something as simple as a cup of white coffee, where white milk has blended with the black coffee to produce a new, connected substance. It can also be as complicated as an orchestra combining the sounds of 50 or more instruments into a harmonious, connected whole. The opposite of harmony is twofold. The first is to be rigid, where interaction is resisted and any movement toward integration is halted. The other is to be chaotic, where elements are in such disarray that it seems impossible to control interaction. Rather than interaction it is more like collisions on one hand and elements flying off out of control on the other.

Our bodies will naturally react to changing circumstances to maintain a stable, harmonious state. Emotionally we prefer to feel a sense of stability, but the reasons why we lose that emotional stability is more complex. Unlike the biological body, which has a set of clear parameters to function within, our emotional stability has to deal with not only reality, but also our memories and our imagined concerns. It is quite easy to create stress and fearfulness. It is not uncommon for us to respond to emotional imbalance with wildly fluctuating behaviours. We can 'freak out' – a chaotic response – or we can refuse to make any change or accept anything new – a rigid response. What we seek, however, is to feel good – to feel in harmony with who we are and what we are doing.

When the body gets too cold or too hot we begin a series of behaviours that act to remedy the problem. These behaviours can be anything from shivering to inventing air conditioning. The elements of the situation interact and produce productive responses by integrating the various elements into a connected and satisfying outcome. Satisfaction is when the outcome is harmonious. From the body perspective, that is when life is preserved and the organism is stable. From the emotional perspective, that is when we feel happy and stable.

Let's think about these compensating actions of the body. Are they a good thing or a bad thing? Certainly they can be uncomfortable and distressing at the time. It may not feel good to be cold and shiver or suffer frostbite, but that is better than losing the use of your internal organs. Bottom line is that we can feel reassuring that we have a natural way of making something happen. When something is happening there is a possibility for change and improvement. What if we apply *the problem is a message* to these compensatory behaviours? From that perspective, shivering is telling us that we are cold; sweating is telling us that we are hot; and perhaps being unhappy is telling that we are doing something that is disturbing to our emotions.

We all know there is nothing unacceptable about shivering when you are cold, but, strangely, there is social disapproval if you have a problem with your emotions. We often either do nothing (rigid) or resist help and let things get out of control (chaos). Rather than being a problem, I suggest that unhappiness is a straightforward message to reconnect, to interact. We are manifesting a feeling that we can notice. The best response is to interact in some way with someone or something. Interaction enables integration and integration seeks harmony. We know this, because all the things that make us feel uncomfortable, painful or disturbed are when things are rigid and/or chaotic.

Dr Daniel Siegel has given a beautiful description of the harmonious state of mind. He has applied his research and theory from a number of disciplines including neuroscience and mathematical complexity theory to arrive at 5 conditions that occur when the brain and the mind are in harmonious state. He uses the acronym F.A.C.E.S.

> **F**lexibility – to be able to make adjustment
> **A**daptability – to adjust to new conditions
> **C**oherence – to make sense of your experience
> **E**nergetic – to feel positive and productive
> **S**table – conditions continue with manageable fluctuation

When our mind is behaving in the way of these 5 qualities, we are in a harmonious state. We know because we feel good about ourselves and happy about our lives. This is the feeling that persists in the creative world and these 5 qualities are the creative world way. If you look back at the 8 Differences you can see their reflection in Dr Siegel's F.A.C.E.S. The first time I heard him speak about this I had goose bumps of excitement the size of basketballs, particularly because I had already written the text of the 8 Differences. It was an inspiring support for the creative world.

The next question is, "How do I know when I am in a F.A.C.E.S. state?" I have invented another acronym that describes how we *feel* when we are integrating in a harmonious direction. Each of these feelings is an indicator that you can use to reassure yourself or warn yourself of the direction you are pursuing in any experience.

Happy – the contented satisfaction of feeling you are
doing what you are meant to do.

Able – having the capability to act.

Responsive – to be empathetically aware and sensitive
in your reactions

Mindful – having an awareness of the present
moment, uninhibited by judgment.

Open – acting with unconditional positive regard

Nascent – sensing that something new is coming into
existence.

Yes – no barrier to what is being created

H.A.R.M.O.N.Y.

If you are feeling all of these things then you know to keep
going. If one or more of these feelings is absent or distressed
then you know to look at what is happening and what messages
these distressed feelings are giving.

I'd like to examine our thinking about harmony a little more
because harmony is important and relevant to a number of
aspects of living:

- Harmony is found when there is a productive co-
  operation of your inner world and outer world. You
  have an innate sense of what is 'right for you' that
  encompasses your inherent dispositions – *the qualities and
  potentials you were born with* - PLUS the developed state of
  mind that comes from experience and your personal
  interaction with that experience – *what your experiences in
  life bring out of you.*

- Harmony can sometimes only be found by swinging
  between rigidity and chaos. This may feel like you are
  out of control and can be quite unsettling in the short
  term. What we now know is that it is very important for
  humans to encounter novel experience in order to

develop the brain and therefore expand the mind and increase our capacity to function successfully. We learn as we go, not just from where we've been.

- The most important aspect of harmony is that it is a direct expression of interaction. Harmony is the relationships between your state of being, your environment and how they are interacting. The emotional indications that you are integrating in a harmonious direction are described in the two acronyms of F.A.C.E.S. and H.A.R.M.O.N.Y. If you are feeling the disturbing effects of the 7 Demons or any of the winner/loser world's 8 Differences, then you are telling yourself that you are not moving toward harmony. So stop and change what you are doing by using any of the 6 Practices. It is as easy as that.

It may even be that conscious efforts to seek harmony are futile in the winner/loser world. I suggest that when we do find harmony in our lives it is because we are acting in the creative world way. In the winner/loser world there is always inhibition to interaction. We transact instead. When you transact there is a desire to draw only the perceived benefits (not integration, but a merger with conditions) and this is done in order to achieve a result that benefits one party at the expense of the other. This will distinguish the winner from the loser. Therefore, in the winner/loser world the opening thought would alter to:

> When elements transact they seek to merge only with beneficial aspects in order to produce a winning result.

The unconditional positive regard required for creative interaction is compromised and therefore harmony remains elusive. The elusiveness of harmony expresses itself as unhappiness and unhappiness affects the whole body and all its systems. It drives us crazy.

✦✦✦ THE PURPOSE OF LIFE ✦✦✦

THOUGHT: *What are we here for? What is the meaning of life?*

This is *the* big question. From the creative world view the answer is quite straightforward. It almost seems too simple to be true, but if you look at this description and consider it without the interference of the 7 Demons and without the inhibition of the 8 winner/loser world Differences, it will seem very reasonable.

- The purpose of life is to creatively participate in the experience and, in doing so, enact the process of creation.

OR, even more simply,

- Life would not be the same without you.

It is your interaction in the experience of life that makes it what it is. It also makes you what you are. Without *you* the experience of life for each and every person would be completely different. The message for anyone contemplating suicide who believes the world can do without them is to consider the 'grain of sand on the beach'. It may well be that if just one grain of sand is taken away then no one will notice, but that is not true. The beach is different. It may be that the difference is very subtle, but it *is* different. The reason why a single grain of sand seems to be so insignificant is because it is so small compared to us.

Think of the universe as a beach full of particles like the sandy beach. Would it really matter, knowing that there are billions and billions of stars (conservatively estimated to be about 10 with 21 zeros after it) and most likely as many or more planets, would it really matter if the Earth was destroyed? I imagine that it would certainly shake up our solar system. The Moon would be very lonely and, realistically it would completely change its orbit and it would wander dangerously around this new gap in the solar system's planetary balance. I also don't think Mars would be able to stay in its current orbit. We are not even mentioning the people. Astronauts on the International Space Station would definitely be a bit freaked out. What would happen when all those radio waves and television signals were finally picked up by extraterrestrial intelligence and they came to search for us? They would be very disappointed to find nothing here. They certainly would have wasted a very long journey.

Every change changes everything. Life would not be the same without any person. It definitely would not be the same without you. This is all, however, dependent on the belief that when things interact there is some kind of beneficially creative process. If you haven't been convinced by the essay on Harmony or by the whole creative world argument, then it might be interesting to consult the great mythologist, Joseph Campbell.

When Joseph Campbell was interviewed by Bill Moyers, he spoke of the benefits of life. These interviews were made near the end of Campbell's life and his wisdom was finely honed. When this topic came up, his response was fascinating:

> People say that what we're all seeking is a meaning for life. I don't think that's what we're really seeking. I think that what we're seeking is an experience of being alive, so that our life experiences on the purely physical plane will have resonances within our own innermost being and reality, so that we actually feel the rapture of being alive.

In another part of the interview he spoke directly on the purpose of life:

> Just sheer life cannot be said to have purpose…(it)
> has a potentiality and the mission of life is to live
> that potentiality.

Campbell called it 'following your bliss'. I believe that the
feelings of H.A.R.M.O.N.Y. are how we know when we are
following our 'bliss'. Experiences simply provide the
opportunity for us to discover, within ourselves, what we have
the possibility to be.

Campbell is saying a number of things here, but one important
aspect is that life is an experience and it is necessary for us to
participate in this experience if we are to truly know ourselves.
When we do participate in the experience we can feel the
relationship between the inner sense of who we could be and
the outer experience where we can express that inner potential.

In psychotherapy we know that when these inner and outer
experiences are in conflict that can cause emotional discomfort
or disturbance. I believe this is largely to do with living in the
winner/loser world. The winner/loser world demands that you
not only win, but win in the areas that have been predetermined
by society to be of value. For most of us that is at odds with our
own inner sense of potential because societal values are often
too limited to generalities and economic needs. We are infected
and debilitated by our struggle to resist the disappointment and
failure that the winner/loser world generates. Some have been
able to resist and even overcome that difficulty and find 'bliss',
but I expect they had to find their own personal creative world.
For many, however, and I believe for an increasing number, the
winner/loser world is just too entrenched and dominating.

This story from Campbell tells it all:

> One fine evening I was in my favorite restaurant
> there, and at the next table there was a father, a
> mother, and a scrawny boy about twelve years old.

The father said to the boy, "Drink your tomato juice." And the boy said, "I don't want to." Then the father, with a louder voice, said, "Drink your tomato juice." And the mother said, "Don't make him do what he doesn't want to do." The father looked at her and said, "He can't go through life doing what he wants to do. If he does only what he wants to do, he'll be dead. Look at me. I've never done a thing I wanted to in all my life."

Even with this rather sad tale of a bliss-less existence, this man's 'grain-of-sand' participation in Campbell's experience has prompted a ripple in life that has extended from Campbell's witnessing of an event to the retelling on television and once again in this book. Life is no longer the same for anyone who reads this page. Having just read that story you have been touched by Campbell, the man, his wife, the boy, the owner of the restaurant, the bank manager that lent the money to start the business, everyone's mother and so on and so on. Chances are you might tell this story to a friend and the whole list of involvement grows. And this is just in relation to a quarter of a page in this book. Life is a very eventful place.

What purpose or meaning of life do we need when we are alive and participating in the experience? If you are living in the moment, mindful of what is happening about you, interacting with your environment and enabling the process of creativity to change the world, then when do you get a moment to wonder why? Every moment produces a new and better experience that brings happiness, harmony and an opportunity to express your potential through your connection with others. The meaning of life is right in front of you. The meaning of life is *you*.

❖❖❖ ZEN AND THE ART OF EVERYTHING ❖❖❖

THOUGHT: *If I say that I will feel better when I am connected, does that mean connected to people or dogs or more than that?*

Zen is a fascinating practice and it has had a good bit of popular treatment in the West. There have been fascinating books such as *Zen and the art of Motorcycle Maintenance,* and other popular insights into Eastern philosophy like the television show *Kung Fu.* Zen ideas have been used in sports, as in archery: *do not just shoot the arrow, be the arrow.*

Zen is actually a name of a particular practice of Buddhism — Zen Buddhism. There are many fascinating ideas and philosophies in this practice, but I want to focus on one rather simple idea — the art of feeling connected to your surroundings.

The idea of *being the arrow* is an attempt to show the archer that he is not separate from the bow or the arrow. Trying to *make* the arrow hit the bulls-eye is to try and dominate and be the controller of the arrow. From a slightly different perspective, it is the arrow that is built to leave the bow and fly to the target. The role of the archer is to create the tension in the bow and be the aim that will allow the arrow to fulfil its purpose. To *be the arrow* is to tune into and interact with the harmonious preference of the arrow to find the bulls-eye. To be in harmony with the arrow means that you must become *connected* to the arrow. It is not about your personal power or control. It is the arrow that must hit the target, not your dominance.

A more western description is to be *in the zone.* Although there may be less spiritual or philosophical aspects to this idea, it is the same sort of thing. A golfer will see the ball going from the putter, along its curve and into the hole. This experience is encouraged in many sports and it was shown that it can even be helpful in looking after a motorbike. Maybe it is a feeling that we could strive to achieve with everything.

Zen and the art of everything relates to the creative world in that by interaction you connect with your environment. Then you can act with an intuitive sense of not only your own harmonious outcome, but also the harmonious outcomes of everyone and everything around you. This may sound like a very complicated thing to do, but remember the act of creativity does not require your controlling influence, only your participation.

As an example: I am lucky to have a holiday house in the Blue Mountains just outside of Sydney which I rent out to holiday makers to subsidise the mortgage. Someone was interested in renting the house for a longer period and I was thinking about whether they should mow the lawn as part of their house-care duties. I then thought about my temperamental old mower and how difficult it is to start. Even my good friend Ben, who is very good with mechanical things, finds it testing. I don't have that much trouble myself, but I was dreading the idea of someone else tugging away at the poor mower and what damage they might do.

What I was really worried about is whether they would understand what the mower needed in order to start. I know that when I am pulling the cord I have concern for its age, as well as a healthy respect. The mower doesn't like to be given single, harsh pulls on the starter cord. It likes to have one long pull, not too fast, and then a few short pulls to keep the motor turning. With a little patience the mower will start and get on with what it is made to do - with a little bit of my guidance and care.

In the winner/loser world the result we're after is to get the blasted mower to do what we want. Men will pull away at the cord like they are controlling a wayward, good-for-nothing reprobate. When the cord finally snaps the air is filled with

144 How the 'real world' is driving us crazy!

curses and criticism about what is at fault and who is to blame. Just replace the image of a mower with any other type of tool and I am sure you can visualise a male you know who has desperately tried to dominate and control some piece of machinery only to break the poor thing and spend the rest of the day cursing everyone and everything under the sun for causing the problem. Now you might also change you image to that of a female who does the same thing with an iron, or perhaps does the opposite of trying to control or dominate by expecting the machine to look after itself. I'm sure you know people who have used some machine to the point of explosion and then heard them reflect on the 'funny noise' they had been hearing for the last half-hour and done nothing about.

Zen and the art of everything is simply about allowing your empathy to extend to all things both animate and inanimate. One of my favourite comments about empathy came from a lecture I did some years ago. We were discussing how we have the amazing capacity to have a true sense of what another person may be feeling. We are indeed able to put ourselves in someone else's shoes. The problem in the winner/loser world is that instead of putting ourselves in their shoes, we try to cram them into ours. I hear this all the time, "I don't understand why she did that!" That, of course, is the point. Not understanding is the *message*, not the problem. In the creative world this is a grand opportunity to learn and grow, and discover what makes other people tick. The problem is *always* a message. The other common saying is to tut-tut disapprovingly and say, "I wouldn't have done that." Of course, we have no idea of exactly what we would have done in that situation and while the "I'm better than you" demon is dominating the experience there is no energy left to understand the other person or learn about life.

What does it feel like to be a book and have your pages turned? How can we participate in the experience of the book? Pages are so easily torn and books so often ruined. We can keep things in good condition by just being careful and respectful. My mother, at 80 years of age, still has possessions from her teenage years. That would be very rare today. Possessions are transient and there for our benefit only. If something breaks you just get another one. Controlling possessions is certainly a lot easier than dominating and controlling people. It is all such a game, but the whole thing is an unwinnable winner/loser world game.

Allowing yourself to imagine that everything has its own contribution to an enjoyable experience changes the disciplinary nature of being careful and respectful to an interactive, responsive connection to everything. The animated film *Toy Story* has a plot that revolves around this concept. The toys were being disregarded and even rejected by the children without any concern for the effect this had on the toys. The toys didn't have any secret agendas or complex characters, they just wanted to be toys and they couldn't really be toys without the children.

To turn the pages of a book because that helps it fulfil its purpose is a strangely satisfying feeling. In the winner/loser world that sort of equality toward other people or other things relegates you from the winner's position and maybe even makes you a loser. In the creative world, however, it turns the mundanity of our daily activities into a resounding coalescence of the desires and needs and wants of everything we encounter. You become a key player and participant in every outcome where each outcome satisfies the desire for harmony and the fulfilment of some purpose. This is how it is for the archer who participates in the bending of the bow, the flight of the arrow, the disturbance of the molecules in the air, the acceptance of the arrow by the target and, then, all these things give back elation to the archer to raise his spirits, not as a winner, but as a part of something far greater than a single, disconnected archer could ever be.

♦♦♦ CONTROL AND POWER ♦♦♦

THOUGHT: *Feeling powerful and winning is very intoxicating. What happens to this feeling in the creative world?*

Being in control is very important in the winner/loser world. It is, however, impossible to control everything. Even when you do all that you can you may still not get a good result. Having to cope with the things that interfere with getting what you want is very frustrating in the winner/loser world. Fault and blame are placed on these 'uncontrollable' elements and the frustration comes out as anger or depression. In the winner/loser world, the 'controller' is never at fault. They are always doing the right things and can't be held responsible. Getting what you want the way you want it is a great way to feel like a winner, but it is dauntingly difficult. Well, it is dauntingly difficult if you set the impossible goal of being in control.

It is not possible to control the creative process. It is not a *thing* that can be manipulated or overpowered. It is simply something that happens when various elements combine. When there is an interaction there will be an outcome that is different from, and in relation to, the elements involved in the interaction. That means that the outcome you get is directly related to the input you give PLUS the input that comes from everything else that is concerned with the interaction that does *not* come from you.

I see this frustration all the time: "I did everything I was asked to do, but the relationship still fell apart". This is, of course, very upsetting, but the interaction was not just about what one person did. In a relationship there are two people, but there are also families, possibly children, work situations, social pressures, problems with the landlord, fluctuations in the economy and all the rest. Certainly, you must do all you can do, but there can never be a *guarantee* that you will get a good result. What the creative world guarantees is that you *will* get an outcome and from this outcome you *will* be able to move on to the next outcome until harmony is re-established.

In the winner/loser world there are so many results that seem to stop you in your tracks. You then have to pull yourself together, re-start the journey and re-establish some momentum. I find this stop/start type of existence very destabilising. It is quite uncomfortable and sets up the frustrations that make us angry and unhappy. The flow of things may vary in the creative world, but there is no reason for anything to stop. There may be a desirable motivation to pause and consider, but this is very different from being stopped.

In popular fiction about lawyers there is often the advice, 'never ask a question you don't already know the answer to'. In the highly adversarial, winner/loser world of lawyers, the purpose of the process is to win. The way to do that is to control and manipulate the evidence that the jury hears. In the jury room the effort is to consider which evidence is credible, which evidence is questionable, and if there is something that can give some unquestionable insight into the truth. In my one experience as a juror, I was amazed at the rationale people used to resolve those issues and find the truth. I can only sympathise with lawyers, especially those who think they have some firm control of the jury. They may try, but there are elements brought by each individual into the jury room that, at least in my case, astonished me. We ended up deciding that the man was not guilty, but it was not anywhere near being a straightforward process. The deliberations in the jury room would have made the lawyers gasp at how ineffective some of their efforts to exert control on the decision actually were.

And so it is with life: when you take an adversarial position and seek to control the situation it can be your very adversarial position that will affect the result beyond your control. When you are trying to force a winning result, there is a natural defensive response from others. Some will become offensive in response to their fear of losing. In the creative world, where you are seeking a harmonious interaction it is much easier. By interacting, rather than transacting, you open up to more possibilities. This means you have a greater chance for an outcome that relates to you and what you desire. This is certainly true in all the areas of the creative world, but especially relationships and families.

In the social structures that have been developed directly from the winner/loser world it is not so easy. Business is largely a winner/loser world structure, but the people within it are not. This causes a friction that is expressing itself today in a massive increase in depression in the workplace. It is necessary to figure out how to be creative in this winner/loser world environment. This can be tricky. There is a special chapter later in this section that talks about business and the creative world that may add more clarity.

So, the bottom line is that you give everything you've got, not because it will guarantee you control and power, but because the greater your energy and input into the interaction then the more desirable the created outcome will be: the more of you there is in an interaction, the more the outcome will be a harmonious expression of you.

♦♦♦ DRUGS ♦♦♦

THOUGHT: *Drugs are the bane of our modern world. What does the winner/loser world have to do with this and can the creative world help?*

This is a very broad and diverse subject with no simple answers or easy understanding. I would, however, like to make some comment that I hope will make a helpful contribution. One of the basic reasons for taking drugs is to 'get out of it'. The world that the drugs create in your mind is better, or at least different, from the one you are in. Sometimes drugs are taken as a form of self-medication. This is very true of alcohol. People just want the pain, discomfort or distressing emotions to go away.

When you look at the circumstances of some people, it is understandable that they want to 'get out of it'. That a lot of these situations are caused by the long-term effects of a winner/loser world culture is probably true, but too complex to discuss here, although I encourage you to think about it. But, there are many people who take drugs for purely recreational reasons. They wish to get out of the space they are in because they are bored or frustrated or just want something else for a change. I'd like to talk about how the winner/loser world might help us understand what motivates and generates a drug culture in the not so desperate and then look at the creative world perspective.

The point of drugs, whether they are illicit, prescription or legally sold over the counter like alcohol and tobacco, is to affect your state of body and mind – to get 'out of it'. Almost all drugs will change the chemical functioning of your brain. This is very disturbing from a health point of view, but obviously not as disturbing as being stuck 'in it'. Getting out of 'it' seems to be worth all the difficulties that come with taking drugs: the expense, the time, the health damage, the other psychological disorders that can be triggered and so much more. So, what is *it*?

It is probably a number of different things: where you are; somewhere you don't want to be; how you are being treated; what you think; what others think of you; how you have to behave; what your position is in the world; how you feel; what you do; your job; your obligations; or just being stopped from doing, thinking or feeling what you want. All these can combine to make an *it* that seems well worth getting away from. Discovering that there were substances you could ingest or inject that would change the chemical landscape in your brain and change your perceptions and perspectives without having to make any personal effort must have been an extraordinary moment. Interestingly, enjoying 'getting out of it' is not necessarily restricted to the human species.

Elephants have been observed to travel lengthy distances following the aroma of ethanol that wafts out of ripening fruit. They are known to enjoy the effects of the fermented fruit (although some of the stories of their drunken escapades on the fruit of the Marula tree are probably exaggerated). Howler monkeys, baboons and various birds have been observed to be drunk on fermented fruit. Wild ring-tailed lemurs enjoy the effects of eating the fermenting Kily lily pods. Elephants have also been known to become aggressive when they consume alcoholic rice beer made by humans (sadly this once led to a group of elephants going on a rampage that killed six people). The slight alcoholic effect that the elephants get from fermenting fruit is dramatically amplified when it is distilled by humans. Just like humans the elephants were unable to cope with the changes to their bodies that concentrated alcohol causes. In the wild, animals have a natural constraint. There is only fruit once a year, so the occasion of a mild alcoholic event is limited and controlled by the natural conditions. Elephants don't have a local bottle shop where they can buy beer. When they stumble across some, they become just as demented and dangerous as humans.

The moral of the elephant story is that when you dramatically change your mind-scape there are going to be a number of effects. Some of these effects are not so enjoyable. Getting out of *it* can land you in a different *it* that is even harder to deal with and control. Alcohol will often trigger aggressive behaviour; amphetamines can give the illusion of great clarity of thought, but it is usually the opposite; cocaine's exciting buzz makes everything move really fast and gets you talking, but mostly you are just a selfish, dominating bore; prescription anti-depressants can ruin your sexuality and interfere with digestion amongst other things; cigarettes give you cancer; needles can give you hepatitis or even AIDS; coming down from the drug can leave you more miserable than before; you can lose the ability to work; children don't get the true love of their parent; you can lose the ability to connect with those you love; you can hurt people; and you can lose your life.

I remember how interesting it was to hear a quote from an older and wiser David Bowie. He said something like, "I don't like to take drugs anymore because what is going on inside my head normally is so much more exciting." The point he is probably trying to make is that drugs can certainly take you to a different place, but why bother when the place you are in is still unexplored and full of possibility. There is a creative world inside your head that can take you anywhere you want without needing any help.

More often than not, I would expect that the world people want to *get out of* is the winner/loser world. *I* want to get out of it. I am lucky that in the period of my life when drugs were readily available I was thoroughly occupied with my outward creative expression. I spent a fortune on hiring recording studios to play music, but it saved me from buying pills and powders. I remember a few years ago being in a queue for a morning cup of coffee. I was enjoying interacting with some of the other people as we waited. One fellow asked, "Hey man, what are you on?" and I was able to honestly reply, "Irrepressible happiness!"

A better way is to get *into* it. This is, quite simply, to creatively participate in life. We take drugs to help us have fun, to relax, to inspire our imagination, to feel affectionate, to get the sex drive going, to make friends, to find truth, but there is not one of those things that is not part of our natural and normal state of being when in the creative world. It is the devastating effects of the winner/loser world problem of disconnection and disengagement that causes the need for something to break the cycle. So, you take something to escape. Trouble is that you end up back where you started, still in the winner/loser world and more of a loser than ever. No wonder the problem is so severe and getting worse.

I haven't mentioned money, yet. I'm sure some of you have thought about it. A lot of people are involved in drugs for the money, not the high. But, for them the money is the high. Money is the measure of a winner, money makes you right and money makes you better. Of course, that is not true from the creative world perspective, but it is true in the winner/loser world. I can't tell you what to choose. It may be that money can bring you happiness, but it has never brought me 'irrepressible happiness'. No matter how much money you win, it will also generate things that make you lose. There is, simply, no permanent or irrepressible form of winning.

Can the creative world change the drug problems of the world? I don't know and I expect that a dramatic change is too much to hope for. As I have said, the drug issue is very complex, but, even still, according to the creative world theory, every new element allows for the possibility of a different outcome. For every person that is able to get rid of the winner/loser world from their heart and mind I believe there can be change.

♦♦♦ RELATIONSHIPS ♦♦♦

THOUGHT: *Relationships are the basic expression of connection and interaction, but the winner/loser world way ruins everything. Even still, living with The Priority Triangle the right way up is surprisingly difficult.*

There is nothing easy about relationships, but there are some basic elements that make a relationship great. The most straightforward is that both partners need to adore each other. The one-sidedness of many relationships predicts difficulty from the start. 'Giving love so that you will get love in return' is another disaster prone belief. For someone to give love to another person on the proviso that they have to love them back is tragically misguided. To be emotionally damaged when it doesn't happen is even more tragic.

The winner/loser world does very little to help relationships. Some relationships might well be able to succeed in an environment where one is the winner and the other is grateful to be under that protection. It can be that the winner role is shared. Stereotypically the male is the dominant winner as the provider and the female is the dominant winner in the home. Nowadays it may even be that the gender role is reversed, but someone dominating somewhere over the other is the general result. This may work to some degree, but it does not guarantee happiness or the unparalleled joy of being adored and being able to adore in return.

In Baz Luhrmann's film *Moulin Rouge* the theme of the love story was given in the immortal line "the greatest thing you'll ever learn is just to love and be loved in return". But the winner/loser world makes this a very difficult quest. In essence, being in love is the perfect expression of the creative world: no conditions, no boundaries, just the combination of two hearts and souls with the desire to create one glorious experience after another. The 'real world' soon takes care of that fantasy!

Let's look at how the 7 Demons interfere with relationships.

Right and Wrong
This is probably the biggest problem that damages the connection between couples. The winner/loser world demands that someone in the relationship be the dominant partner and the most common indicator is who is right. Most arguments are about this issue.

Even when something has been decided you will hear one or other say, "Yes, but I just want you to acknowledge that what I said was right, even though I am agreeing to what you want." Unless the other partner agrees there can be a continuing tension. Even if there is acknowledgement that one partner has an agreeable point it is often not believed unless the other partner actually does what has been said. This escalates the problem because that partner is feeling that their opinions are not respected. The end result is that both partners think they are being browbeaten into how they should think and how they should live.

Both think of themselves as losers and both fight to feel more like a winner. The stupid thing is that it is the *fight to be right* that becomes the problem. Fighting is a huge Catch-22: nobody wins, especially children. It can become very damaging for the children when they are used as pawns to win the argument. The frustrating thing for a therapist is that it can sometimes be very difficult to overcome this need to be right. Even when it is obviously causing a great deal of harm, there is a part of our mind that believes that being wrong is a threat to our wellbeing. Being wrong may even damage the wellbeing of our children or loved ones. Some people continue to believe this even when the damage being caused is obvious. The damage is always someone else's fault. This elevates *being right* into being a moral and just cause. It becomes a crusade. Like any crusade, to fight on regardless of 'collateral damage' is just a little crazy.

Good and Bad.
This demon concerns how you feel about the way things work out. Because the winner/loser world is based in results, there is an end point that can be examined, assessed and reacted to with a good or bad feeling. This becomes damaging because it breaks down life into a series of events rather than an ongoing process. In the creative world way it is easier to look upon an outcome as something that is pleasing or something that needs

continuing work. An undesired outcome can help by pointing toward something that might be a better idea or approach.

An immediate reaction to feeling negative about a bad result is to start looking for whom to blame. These demons work hand in hand and sometimes it can feel like a relay: just when you think you have things under control the baton is passed to another demon and the whole situation can flare up again. The flare up can even be about something entirely different because the demons can bring unconnected problems together.

Why we feel better by defeating someone with whom we have a caring relationship is the question that bothers so many people. The winner/loser world theory shows that driving a wedge between relationships is a predictable probability. Not so in the creative world where the preservation of connection is the basic foundation.

Feeling bad about how something has worked out defines the situation and makes it a bad event. An event has no further development. It is an end point, rather than a creative springboard. An event can take a specific place in memory and be recalled as something specific that can be used as a reference point. The effect of this system in a relationship is a build up of problems that can be used in the present for power or control or to simply get the upper hand. How many times have you heard or said, "We're not doing that again…" or "Last time we did this you ruined everything…" or "If you expect me to go through this again you've got another thing coming…"

The conversation should be about what has been learnt, how to do things better, examining why the situation has occurred again. The creative world gives you systems that take you forward and allow for a loving process to persist even in the face of difficulty. That is why we relate to others: to make life easier in co-operation and friendship.

Expectation

When you enter a relationship with someone because of what you expect, trouble is already on your doorstep. I am surprised at the number of troubled couples who tell me that their partner has never changed and still does all the things that they hate. This is a major dilemma for that person: If I am the same as I always have been then what did you expect? In many ways they have a good point, not that that excuses people who make others unhappy.

It seems to be a more common complaint from women about men. The issue may be that some women have the idea that they might marry a boy, but he will soon turn into a man. This does happen to many men, but, unfortunately, not all. From the male perspective the biggest problem I come across is men who expect their wife to look after them just like their mother did. These are the extreme ends of expectation, but they are common enough to have touched most of us. These expectations are unrealistic, unreasonable and, frankly, terribly shallow. There are so many other expectations that are hidden into our culture and when they are not met the couple feel like losers.

I'm sure you can think of many examples and they usually begin with 'should': he should bring in plenty of money; she should do all the housework; he should know how to fix things; she should look sexy all the time; he should settle down and stop playing with his mates; she should organise all the social activities; and so it goes.

Sometimes the list of expectations that someone has for a partner becomes a fanciful impossibility. When your partner doesn't 'measure up' then the relationship feels like a waste of time and you need to get rid of the 'loser'. It's heartbreaking. Expectations can even stop the partner from developing because they don't want to be told what to do. Again we enter a cycle where we destroy any possibility of creating a life together.

To be alive and to be together is an excellent start. The rest is full of possibility and is a great adventure. The best thing to expect is that you never know what to expect, except love.

Fault and Blame

The winner/loser world *demands* that someone is at fault. It is hard to resist. Even when someone gallantly accepts blame it is often against their inner feelings. I have seen many couples where one partner will accept the blame just to keep the peace. Slowly they build up a resentment that tears them apart. It is a common joke that the best thing a man can learn to say is "Yes, dear". This is largely because women have to make such an effort to be noticed in a world where men have inherited the dominant role.

The creative world way could be something more like, "That's interesting dear. Tell me everything you're thinking about this and let's see what we can create together." You may be having a little giggle now at the idea of such an exchange. How often do people talk like that? The bigger question is, why *don't* we?

Fault and blame either slow down or even completely halt any progress. It may seem gallant or even prudent to accept blame or boldly accuse, but it just takes the energy out of things when you do. When fault is accepted or given there has to be a period of submission, then there is often a period of punishment and sometimes recompense. A great deal of time is spent finding equilibrium again and directing the momentum in a better direction.

In fictional drama we often see the story of the distressed couple under enormous amounts of pressure. They keep everything to themselves because no one wants to look like they can't handle their own problems. The situation escalates until there is a flash point. Suddenly the couple see the error of their ways and embrace each other with greater passion. It almost looks as though their pig-headed stupidity was good for the relationship. The reality is that mostly people break under these pressures and the flash points are usually when the relationship splits, someone gets hurt or even worse. The key to romantic fiction is that the characters hold their emotions close to their chest. This builds up dramatic tension, but the writer knows how the drama is going to play out. In life we can never be so sure.

Somehow we have to break the cycle of disengagement and also the myth of pushing something until it breaks. Here's a crazy idea to think about: If your relationship is suffering from a lot of arguments, then next time you have an argument start taking off your clothes (at home, I suggest, not in the supermarket). I don't know exactly what will happen, but I can assure you that the argument will be altered, especially if you disrobe with a bit of 'attitude'. Of course, if the situation gets worse you should stop. I am not asking you to place yourself in a position of being naked and humiliated, but if things take a frisky turn for the better, then maybe you can test the idea of *make love not war*. What else can we do to remind ourselves that life is for living and relationships are for loving? We must continue to try and break the cycle of winning and introduce the idea of creatively loving.

Criticism
I don't think I need to say anything much here. Who hasn't been the butt of, or the giver of criticism? It is the quickest and easiest way to shift the blame. It puts the other person on the back foot. The instinctive reaction to criticism is the same as if physically attacked: people defend. Couples can find themselves in a terrible row because each believes they are simply defending themselves. He said, she said… It is common knowledge that a man should never tell the truth if his partner asks whether they look nice. There are so many winner/loser world complexities expected, that it is better to say some meaningless platitude. That is a great shame. It means that a genuine compliment is lost amongst the charade of avoiding a 'criticism fight'.

The damaging power of criticism is expressed in the way it pushes the other person down, makes them feel like a loser. Criticism specifies just why someone is not 'good enough' and doesn't 'measure up'. This, however, begs the question, "Good enough for what?" The answer is multi-layered: good enough in the eyes of others; good enough to look like a winner; good enough to be better than someone else; good enough not to be as bad as someone else. I could go on, but all these values are based on some judgement made by others, about others and to satisfy others. This single issue could fill another book.

To criticise is mostly about tearing down. We talk about constructive criticism, but the trick is to be sure that the other person realises that it is not them as a person being criticised, but something about what they are doing. This is very difficult. In the winner/loser world it is *very* difficult. When what you do is just an extension of your value as a person, then criticism will damage *you* in some way. The creative world way is not to criticise by finding what is wrong, but by examining whether the outcome is desirable or undesirable. This is the same as looking to see if the process is integrating in a harmonious direction. Just use the H.A.R.M.O.N.Y. measure, then seek to take the process to the next level and then the next level and so on. In the creative world you can become so busy looking at what is interesting and allowing for the next creative outcome, that it seems silly to pause for criticism.

Isolation

I never cease to be amazed at how many people in relationships are lonely. They may even spend a great deal of time with their partner or other friends, but there is no feeling of connection and so, they feel alone. Dr 'Patch' Adams, the famous clown doctor, considers that a more honest diagnosis of depression would be loneliness. He insightfully suggests that it is very difficult to be depressed when you are thinking of about a friend at the same time. Loneliness peppered with boredom and fear is what can happen when you don't have deeply meaningful, sweet, loving relationships with friends.

It is not only possible, but also likely that people will feel disconnected from other people in the winner/loser world. The fact that we make so much effort to maintain and re-establish connection shows how important it is to us all. In relationships we can find an island of relief or an oasis of connection in the winner/loser world. In relationships we can experience love and love is a creative process of unconditional positive regard. For as long as you can maintain a loving position you can be immune to the disturbance of the winner/loser world. That, unfortunately, doesn't mean you will be unaffected by the demands of the winner/loser world. It means that you have increased the possibility that you will intuitively adopt the creative world ways.

Guilt
Guilt is an extension from the 'should' of expectation to 'how can I make amends'. The principal feeling of guilt is shame. Guilt burdens you with both responsibility and a demand that you fix the problem. The classic storyline in a romantic novel is when the man forgets the birthday or anniversary and the women must be spoilt with presents and special attention to make up for the failing. Men are also known to highlight their partners failing and use this to get the 'royal treatment'. Women can also do it to each other by using criticism and expectation to shame a woman into feeling she is not a good housewife or mother and, nowadays, not getting a good enough job.

Shame is an awful feeling and it can be triggered by almost all of the other demons. That is why guilt is such a distressing emotion and also so common. The beautiful, shared interaction that is the pleasure of being in a relationship is impossible to maintain in an atmosphere of guilt and shame. This is especially true for children. We do terrible damage to young people when we try to shame them into doing what is expected of them. I am a father and I understand how hard it is to raise children, to help them, protect them and give them the best advantage in life. We cannot allow shame and guilt to interfere with these worthy outcomes, but that is a difficult task in a winner/loser world environment.

It is, unfortunately, necessary to prepare our children (and ourselves) for the existence of the winner/loser world social structures, systems and behaviours, but that doesn't mean that we have to make our homes a winner/loser world, too. If we are to have an island of refuge as we try to change to a creative world way, then let it be the home with people we love. That is what relationships are all about – the sharing of love, not the teaching of hardship.

I heard someone say once, "Children need hugs when they deserve them the least". This saying is accepting that the disruptive behaviour can be a message more than a problem. It can be an expression of needing connection rather than deserving to be punished. Certainly Dr 'Patch' Adams endorses the idea that 'when in doubt, give a hug'. I believe that this is something that can be practiced regardless of age, sex, religion or politics. When in doubt, make a connection. It may not be a great big bear hug, but to touch, to be close or to attend another person with tenderness. These are all simple things we can all do. The winner/loser world may *seem* to allow us to be close at times, but not close enough to matter. To me it always matters, but we seem to have devised ways to be in a close environment, but remain separate and disengaged.

The *cherry on the top of the triangle* is to put loving relationships at the pinnacle of our motivation. In the creative world, that is obvious. In the winner/loser world love is often left waiting until all the other problems have been solved and conquered. The way relationships struggle nowadays I believe that it is self evident that satisfying the winner/loser world first simply does not work.

✦✦✦ FINDING THE ENERGY FOR LIFE ✦✦✦

THOUGHT: *Why do we feel more energetic during creative activity?*

Trying to feel 'on' or 'pumped' or 'motivated' all the time is not easy. It is probably impossible. Winners like to feel they are 'pumped'. You see this on television as 'winners' motivate the hell out of us with fixed grins, fabulous bodies and unrelenting energy. If being bouncy and energised is the opposite of tired and lethargic, then I guess some people might think that is the answer. But is 'unrelenting energy' such a good thing? The fact that it is unsustainable in the long term means that it cannot be an essential element of feeling good or of being happy. So, the feeling of positive energy, even though it may *include* the feeling of being 'pumped', is something else. It must be something that is more easily achieved and able to be continuous. Happiness and feeling energy for living cannot be about how much you jump up and down or rush about. It is about the absence of resistance as you move through the experience of life.

For many people who try to be vibrantly happy all the time there is the inevitable let down. Feeling less than vibrantly happy causes a fear that something is wrong. This is an enormous pressure for people to place on themselves, but is a common misinterpretation of the energetic state. In the state of meditation there is strong feeling of having energy without any activity. The outward show of vibrant energy can well become a winner/loser world issue: I am more bouncy than you are!

So, why do we feel more energetic during creative experiences? Because when we are creatively participating in our experience in the creative world there is little or no resistance to the process. There is, of course, creativity in the winner/loser world, but it is limited and inhibited by resistance caused by winner/loser world expectations.

People drive themselves crazy trying to write a successful novel or sing in tune. Some hide in the background so as not to be in a position of criticism. In the winner/loser world the outcome is affected by the winner/loser paradigm. It is just so much more fun and so much more pleasurable and productive in the creative world. That is why it feels more energetic.

The answer is concerned with the nature of the creative experience. Creativity is not something you do or don't do. It is simply the name we give to what is going on when things are integrating. The question is why are some experiences energising and others tiring? It is important to note that at some stage we will get tired. The body can only do so much. There are also simple biological issues, like the available body sugar, blood flow, muscle strength and the other things that contribute to physical tiredness.

The energy we are talking about is more to do with a state of mind, a feeling. Some people can climb Mount Everest and feel exhilarated, whereas others can walk down the hall and feel not only exhausted, but miserable. This is directly related to the way you *feel* about what you are doing and what it means to you to achieve it. The amount of interference, resistance and discouragement that exists in your life will deplete the amount of energy that is used up in the process. There is a more theoretical look at this idea in Section 3.

Basically, everything has its own 'energy'. Everything has molecules and atoms that have energy so, whether it's one atom or billions in a 'clump', everything has energy of some sort. When elements interact they will seek to integrate. This integration will bring the energy of the individual elements together and their energy will combine. If there is no resistance then the energy of the outcome will be a combination of the energy of the elements that interact. Any resistance will reduce that energy. So, what is the resistance?

Resistance comes in many forms, but the most important are in our thoughts and emotions. All your negative beliefs about yourself interfere with the creative process. Emotional traumas that are still unresolved interfere. The biggest interference is the winner/loser world imposition of needing to win and fearing to lose. Traumas and injuries in your body can interfere, but even more so if you *believe* that you are damaged goods. (I'm sure there are lots of other things you can think of. I hope you are writing these in the margins.) In the winner/loser world there is a *lot* of resistance. There will be some resistance in the creative world too, but there you can use *the problem is a message* to become aware of unresolved issues and enlarge the experience with *what can I create* into a much broader healing experience.

The most damaging resistance of them all is being in control. When you *try* to make something happen; when you *manipulate* the circumstances toward a pre-determined result; when you *try* to be just like the fabulously motivated energy-ball on the TV, you will find, as so many do, that it is just exhausting and the results are hard to enjoy – if you do at all.

Can it really be enough to simply have fun? Can you do anything worthwhile and have fun in the process? Can there be pleasure in doing hard work? These questions only exist in the winner/loser world. In the creative world you are having too much fun and pleasure to think about such things.

Think of something that you have done that was exhausting and even though you got the result you wanted, wasn't satisfying. What were the barriers? What got in the way? What drained the energy from the experience before you even got to the end result? If you aren't sure of the answers, you might like to review the 8 winner/loser world Differences and the 7 Demons before asking the questions again. I expect that you will find the answers. In the answers you will discover the problems. Of course, these problems are only messages in the creative world. Listen to the message and create something better.

✦✦✦ FAMILY DYNAMICS ✦✦✦

THOUGHT: *Being in a family can be a pleasure, but it can also be very difficult. Everything can get so much more complicated.*

Families have a distinct and unique type of relationship. One of the most obvious differences is that you can't leave your family. You can try. You may think you have, but you never do. Even people who don't know they have other family can feel that something is missing in their lives.

A client told me that she was not speaking to her brother and hadn't done so for five years. She had put it behind her and had no problems with it at all. I asked her what else she was doing five years ago. She remembered that, amongst other things, she changed jobs around that time. I asked her how many of the people she used to work with were not speaking to her any more. Of course she replied that no one was 'not speaking' to her, she hadn't seen or heard form any of them in years. She had gone on to other things. "Just like your brother?" I suggested. "Well, yes, but no, not really…" she stumbled.

She had no thoughts about the people from work because they were no longer included in her life dynamic. Her brother, on the other hand was a prominent issue that she spoke about almost as soon as the session began, despite the fact that she was convinced she was unaffected. You can't sack your family, like workmates or acquaintances. They are part of your experience. The number of relatives included in an active family dynamic depends on the culture of the individual family, but it can range from just parents and siblings to a host of cousins, aunts, uncles and in-laws. Whatever the nature of your family, the people included in the dynamic are a constant element of your life.

Families have an unwritten hierarchy. Grandparents to parents, older siblings to younger siblings, blood family to in-laws. This can be very frustrating when the youngest child is expected to do the dirtiest job even when they are 45 years old. Christmases are strewn with stories of family gathering disasters when the family hierarchy is revived. Whatever problems may exist remain until they are resolved. Whatever psychological disturbances may exist within individuals or between family members will continue to affect the family dynamic.

The winner/loser world paradigm finds a real home in families. The 7 Demons can wreak havoc because no one can escape. It is, of course, also the perfect place for the creative world to flourish. It is the obvious place of relationship. It is up to the family to discover which world they wish to be in.

Being 'stuck' with your family leaves open the temptation to maintain or gain some advantage. Guilt is a huge player in family dynamics. Expectation can send younger family members into fits of stress and depression. Watching fault and blame being flung about in a dysfunctional family can be like watching tennis. The idea is to acknowledge this minefield, accept that it is the place where your family will always play and seek to clear the dangers, one by one.

When families are in trouble it is best for them to work together. If there is serious trouble and professional help is needed, then it is always good to try and deal with it together. If you can't do this then even if only one person is working through the issues the changes in that family member will have some effect. From the creative world perspective it is important to create with what is available. There is no benefit in demanding how things *should* be and complaining about how they *would be if only*... A useful therapy to start with is *The Priority Triangle*. The outcome to be seeking is that there is a priority of love. As difficult as it may seem, the demon of *expectation* needs to be banished. Each individual member of the family can only be who they are.

The most disruptive temptation within families is to give advice. Mostly, when advice is given, the advice is expected to be taken. When advice is ignored the giver often feels disrespected and not taken seriously. On the other hand the person being given advice doesn't want to take it and look as though they are stupid, even if the advice is good. This is a grand winner/loser world trap and families everywhere fall into it every day. This is not because the advice isn't useful, just that it is often interpreted as instruction rather than information.

Competition is often an open sore that festers on the surface of family dynamics. Everyone holds, and sometimes grasps, the events of the past. Fights that were lost years ago can sit festering in a family member's heart just waiting for the chance to get some payback. It sounds sad, but true and not at all surprising in the winner/loser world. So much of growing up seems to be unfair. Strangely the concept that life is fair, or even-handed, comes from the winner/loser world and then the actual unfairness of the winner/loser world creates a destructive friction.

The resolution of these issues is probably very hard to find in the winner/loser world. Families intuitively embrace the creative world when they lift their love for each other up to the 'cherry on top' of the priority triangle. From the creative world view, the connection between family members is a basic aspect of our species and means that it is with family that we have to work even more thoughtfully to avoid the terrors of the 7 Demons and pay close attention to the way the 8 Differences are allowed to impact. The family is a place of learning, it is a place of inescapable interaction and most importantly, it is a place of belonging. Making this experience happy and enriching is not an easy task, but it is so much easier in the creative world.

◆ PSYCHOTHERAPY IN THE CREATIVE WORLD ◆

THOUGHT: *If you live the creative world way does that mean there is no need for psychotherapy?*

I believe psychotherapy to be an invaluable tool and will continue to be even when we all adopt the creative world way. In the creative world, psychotherapy is a very creative tool. The problem with psychotherapy in the winner/loser world is that although we help people to gain their feet, we put them back in a winner/loser world that just knocks them down again.

Thinking in psychotherapy is, however, moving away from the "what's wrong with you" therapy and strongly adopting the "what's right with you" approach, which is very much a creative world paradigm. Carl Rogers introduced his *person-centred* techniques in 1951. He was a pioneer in the suggestion that we should approach people as being basically good, but unable to *actualise* their potential. What I suggest is that the biggest interference to our ability to *actualise* ourselves, or express our potential, is the constraint of the winner/loser world ways.

There is a powerful movement toward a more positive style of psychotherapy that looks to create happiness. Not only does it look to create happiness, but to use happiness as a cure. Dr William Glasser, developer of Reality Therapy and Choice Therapy, finds that he astounds his patients when he helps them resolve complicated issues by simply helping them to be happy.

In a number of his books, Dr Glasser also talks about an 'external world' which makes happiness very difficult. I believe we are on a very similar wavelength. I believe the winner/loser world and Glasser's 'external world' are founded on the same realisations. He has communicated to me that he also recognised some similarities. I take great comfort to receive such caring encouragement from such an esteemed member of the psychotherapeutic community.

The idea of the winner/loser world theory and the winner/loser world problem is to provide an understanding platform to help us alter the belief system that winning *must* be the dominant force in human experience. As I have stated a number of times, winning is a normal desire and a part of our instinctive behaviour. Connection and integration are also normal desires and necessary aspects of human survival and happiness. We may not be able to get rid of the winner/loser world easily because it is entrenched in our economic systems and our social structures, but we can certainly take it 'off the pedestal'.

Psychotherapy in the context of the creative world becomes a grand and exciting adventure. To practice therapy of the emotions and the mind in an environment where happiness is a desired and acceptable outcome will be very rewarding. Even in a creative world there will be trauma and there will be difficulties that need special attention. There will also be plenty of healthy winning and losing experiences that will need to be processed and resolved. There will be more than enough to do. Hopefully we will stop feeling as though we are beating our heads against a brick wall – the winner/loser wall.

A buzzword in psychotherapy today is 'integration'. This concept is of vital relevance now as we come to grips with the idea that our entire system is connected. Everything from the tip of our toes to the top of the head has mechanisms that communicate and connect. *All* of the body interacts with *all* of the rest of the body. This interaction produces an integration that increases our awareness of our self. Much of this integration is not on a conscious level. Nobody suddenly sits up and says, "Ah, my liver has just had an interaction with a neuro-peptide which is enabling a beneficial process that lets my brain produce positive neuro-transmitters that give me a more positive mood." We don't have conscious realisations like this, but we don't need to. There are plenty of other things for our conscious mind to think about and notice. Our internal housekeeping looks after itself as we are attracted by the novelties that excite us and inspire our thoughts.

Dr Daniel Siegel takes the process of integration even further to include other people. His work is broadly titled, 'Interpersonal Neuro-Biology'. This is wonderful work that illuminates our understanding of the processes of integration concerning the human brain and mind. He also describes the effects of integration with other brains and minds. This is the first realistic description of a communal mind and perhaps even a universal mind. Without the need for magical or unknown intervention we can simply gather together and create a mind that is greater than ourselves. All we need to do is come together.

Dr Martin Seligman has researched and developed a system of psychotherapy that is simply called 'Positive Psychotherapy'. He gives a wonderful perspective on the value of happiness and how we can express this in our life. He looks at life experience on three levels: the Pleasant Life; the Engaged Life; and the Meaningful Life. His focus is very much oriented in the creative world way. The Pleasant Life consists of thinking and feeling positively about our past, present and future until we are experiencing life at the top of our potential. The Engaged Life grows when we work with our strengths and alter our lives toward these strengths. The Meaningful Life is when we use our strengths and talents to serve something greater than ourselves. In the context of the creative world, we are involved in something greater than ourselves as soon as we include others in our experience. All we need to do is reject the dis-integration of the winner/loser world and embrace the creative world path of connection and interaction.

There are numerous other wonderful exponents of psychotherapy that have realized the value of the human desire to connect. There are many different styles of therapy that endeavour to bring the strengths within you to the surface and help you resist the constant barrage of winner/loser world defeatism. The only thing that no one seems to have done is to name and describe the winner/loser world as a concept. In understanding the existence of the winner/loser world and the emotionally destructive pattern of the winner/loser world problem we can stop the processes of damage.

It seems apparent from what is happening in the world that therapy can be less than helpful if you are unaware of the existence of the winner/loser world or the winner/loser world problem. Providing an oasis or an island that relieves people from the stress of the winner/loser world problem only gives temporary relief. As soon as you leave, all the fabulous lessons and experiences lose their relevance and effectiveness because you are back in the thick of the winner/loser world again.

I am, however, heartened to think that many people experience their personal version of the creative world and intuitively understand the existence of the winner/loser world. That is why there is still happiness in the world, despite the apparent fall of many into unhappiness. This only goes to show that living in the creative world is possible and more than that, do-able. I believe that this book will allow those that haven't been able to intuitively see the false reality of the winner/loser world to feel the 'penny drop'. Many will find that they already use many of the creative world skills and will know instantly how to make these experiences permanent and independent of the winner/loser world problem. Others will do this in time. Some will learn it for the first time. Sadly, I expect that there will also be those who neither 'get it' nor even choose to, but this is the nature of human choice.

Meanwhile, I look forward to a psychotherapy practice where the barriers are down or, at least, easier to overcome. I look forward to many of the irrational beliefs that we have battled for so long simply disappearing, ceasing to have relevance, losing their personal affect. I look forward to people being as happy as they are naturally, creatively designed to be.

◆◆◆ BUSINESS AND BUCKS IN THE ◆◆◆
CREATIVE WORLD

THOUGHT: *If business is based in the winner/loser world does that mean that creative world people can't be involved?*

The immediate response may be to think that creative world people cannot be involved in anything as winner/loser as business. The insight of the 'winner/loser world theory' is that we do not have to exclude anything from our experience in order to be happy. The purpose of this book is to re-establish that your worth as a human being is not based on whether you satisfy the winner/loser world. For the creative world person it is completely possible to participate in business and the generation of money as a creative experience, rather than a self-worth experience.

Imagine waking up, feeling wonderful and relishing the prospect of participating in the experiences of the day, regardless of what they might be. What if the enjoyment of your day is not dependent on whether it is work or recreation or mowing the lawn or meeting friends or making a deal with a prospective client? That is the creative world experience.

This is not to say that there will not be some tension and stress. Tension and stress are very healthy in energising our motivation responses. If, however, the process – whatever it is – makes you feel awful and sends you down a destructive spiral of prolonged stress and low self-esteem, then the question must be asked: "What is the problem?" The problem then needs to be seen as a message where something can be done both *about* it and *with* it.

We do not have to live miserable lives because the economy demands it or because there is a 'real world' out there. What we must do is *create* a liveable world that includes the concept of an economy AND the greater concept of *enjoyment of life*.

There is nothing new in this. In fact we have had a vast number of tools at our disposal for some time. Undoubtedly the most influential proponent of the creative process is Edward de Bono. He has pioneered the idea of creativity in all aspects of life. There is no one who has done it better. That said, it is still necessary to point at the business world and declare it to be a system that is based on winner/loser principles. Economic rationalism with all its targets, focus points and 'bottom line' demands finds it difficult to include the human element. An economy may not be based on people, but business is staffed by people and its produce is consumed by people. Business has always been about people. Sadly it has also been about the manipulation of people.

It seems to me that the winner/loser world strategies (which are expressed in the 8 Differences and the 7 Demons) are the cause of many of our business and workforce troubles. These problems affect performance, productivity, job satisfaction and company loyalty. We seem to be throwing a lot of effort and money at this to try and fix it, but if the problem with business is the way that business affects people, then no amount of money hurling is going to fix it. In fact the money is not only going to waste, it is probably making the problem worse.

We must address the way we approach the value of people in business. We must address the way we apply pressure to perform. We must address the way we believe that achieving targets is the measure of a person's worth.

People *are* the value of a business. It doesn't matter how many buildings are owned, they are empty without the people. It doesn't matter how successful your bottom line is if the cost is human misery. It doesn't matter how many targets are met if people burn out and have to be replaced. Hiring and training are such expensive exercises. There is no reason why participation in business cannot be a fulfilling life experience on a day-to-day basis. What is required is a 'bottom line' of fulfilment for the people in your business.

What are the big problems in business today?
1. maintaining productivity
2. maintaining enthusiasm
3. staff turnover

Points 2 and 3 just add to the magnitude of point 1 and all three are affected by the human response to prolonged stress. One of the main complaints I hear is that people become frustrated and angry. They don't feel that they are able to express their concerns and when they do they are not listened to. The job becomes dull and routine; performance pressures are unrealistic and 'inhuman'; and private pleasure is both affected by time and the inability to relax. In short, people suffer the ill effects of a winner/loser world.

The biggest buzzword in business at the moment is 'innovation'. There is a lot of energy being put into having innovative staff and innovative development of the company. Lots of money is being spent trying to teach people how to be creative and inventive; how to take productive initiative; how to become better team players. All of these are excellent goals. De Bono has been showing people how to do this for decades and we are still trying to achieve it. The problem is that it is very difficult to change the 'winner' approach from within the winner/loser world. Creativity and team play is not compatible with individual competition for rewards. There can be no real innovation until there is genuine engagement of the people involved. Find me a group of employees who truly trust each other. Possible, but not common.

I was reading a website of a group that teaches companies how to be innovative. A satisfied client reported the wonderful changes that had been brought. The managing director spoke about one department where there were several teams. Before the innovation training, these groups would hardly speak to each other, and were very guarded about any developments being made. He was pleased to report that after the training, this department had learnt how to combine and create an enjoyable workspace, so much so that he was receiving unsolicited applications for transfers to this department.

I think this is a wonderful story, but doesn't it set off a few alarm bells? How is it possible that the most social and interactive species on this planet can find themselves in a position where 24 people are unable to work together in an open, trusting and productive way? The answer, of course, is because that is what the winner/loser world does to us. This single example shows that something can be done, but it also shows that an enormous amount is yet to be done. We have to lift ourselves out of the dark ages and *then* we might be able to enter the creative world.

Structuring business in a creative world way may require radical changes in some areas, but mostly, it can be quite subtle. When people begin to operate in the 8 creative ways then the negative effects of the 7 Demons will largely disappear. When these negatives are not involved in the process the entire situation improves immediately. The difficulty may be in *believing* that this will work. We continue to stay with the devil we know - just in case. But just in case of what? The alternative possibilities need to be shown and made available.

Here are some suggestions for business practice in a creative world environment:
- *team* targets, which are achieved through individual *contribution:* the capacity for each individual is based on their potential rather than their fear of failure.
- co-operative interaction rather than competitive reward
- acknowledgement of *effort* as well as *results*
- education, training and/or support when effort is not succeeding in producing results

- understanding and acknowledgement of the natural talents of individual team members so they can be utilised effectively and efficiently
- applying individual talents to create a multi-faceted team, just like a sports team that has different positions for different body types and talents.
- acknowledgement of the actual results as well as their relationship to target expectations
- open-ended goals that allow for achievement *greater* than set targets
- broader understanding by everyone involved of what the company is doing and what it is aiming for, rather than just disembodied performance targets
- regular training and practice in interpersonal skills
- regular training and practice in communication skills
- regular 'innovation' processes and workshops
- regular forums where people can share non-critical conversation and/or counselling
- acknowledging the positive human outcome – what has been created and what might be created
- transparency in the process of how ideas and suggestions are considered
- every idea utilised in some way. Even unworkable ideas are productive in what they can inspire. This can happen in the 'innovation workshops'.
- problems examined for their message and improvements investigated
- incorporation of existing creative techniques eg. De Bono's 6 hats, the 6 Practices
- frustration corner – a place for discussion and dissipation of frustrated energy as well as positively redirecting frustrated energy
- creating a motivated environment for innovation and enjoyment

- changing the process of selling into a process of personal satisfaction for both the seller and the buyer
- to remove the barriers, constraints and restrictions so that the experience really is satisfying

To achieve these outcomes may take time and will certainly take effort, but the very effort that is required will begin to accumulate energy. This is, of course, if the energy is not wasted on frustrating interference, constraints and restrictions.

When there is an interaction, everything plays a part. There is no different in business. When business issues are involved in the interaction these are relevant. The creative world way is to allow everything into the mix. That means the needs of the business *and* the needs of the people. We have already discussed how people will seek a harmonious outcome and we have an easy to remember acronym to measure this. If you remember, the human indication of harmony is expressed in the acronym of feeling: **H**appy, **A**ble, **R**eceptive, **M**indful, **O**pen, **N**ascent, **Y**es.

Business has its own indicators that things are moving in a *businesslike* harmonious direction. This can be captured in another acronym. Essentially a business needs to be:

> **H**elpful – to both staff and customer.
> **A**ctive – in the promotion and production of its product
> **P**roductive – in a qualitative and efficient manner
> **P**rofitable – spending less than what is earnt
> **I**nnovative – finding better ways to do things
> **N**ecessary – satisfying some purpose or need
> **E**xpanding – maintaining sustainable growth
> **S**ensitive – to the needs of customers and staff
> **S**table – to avoid unacceptable risks

H.A.P.P.I.N.E.S.S.

When we create an environment where a business is able to positively express its H.A.P.P.I.N.E.S.S and at the same time the worker is able to feel the positive message of H.A.R.M.O.N.Y., we will discover a creative business world. Business structures will naturally evolve conditions and systems that will reflect and support a creative, innovative workplace. To say that it is too late to change these institutions is to forget that *we* made them in the first place, and to forget that we are preparing a life for our children. Let us not give our children a world that is impossible to enjoy and unbearable to endure.

♦♦♦ SELF-ESTEEM ♦♦♦

THOUGHT: *So many people feel so badly about themselves or have been led to believe they are of little value.*

This is such a common problem. So many people simply feel as though they are not good enough. This can be for a multitude of reasons. When you stop and look at what happens to people every day, it is a wonder that we have any esteem at all.

Everywhere you turn there is something that feels like a critical comment. Beautiful, retouched faces adorn magazine covers; you drive past a car that you have always wanted, but can't afford; someone at work gets a promotion; a friend's exciting story about their weekend makes you feel like your life is dull; a pimple breaks out on your face; someone makes a thoughtless and hurtful remark; you see your ex-partner with someone else; the food you just bought for a quick lunch tastes like cardboard; your mother rings and tells you what you haven't done; not one person has smiled at you all day; your credit card bill has blown out of all proportion; and that is just this morning!
I hope that not everyone's day is quite like that, but these things are the sorts of things that happen on a regular basis and they

just whittle you down. When you begin to notice these 'negative' things more readily than the 'positive' things in your life, your low self-esteem has entered a self-fulfilling dynamic. It can be very hard to pull yourself out. That is when friends come to your aid; however, I have talked with people that feel bad about the fact that someone is helping them. This is when recovery becomes almost impossible.

The reason why negative feelings seem to grow is now better understood. Put simply, what you *notice* determines which part of your brain is activated. The part of your brain that is activated determines the types of chemicals and neural pathways that are activated. If you notice 'negative' things then the aspects of you brain that respond create an unhappy mood. If most things that you notice support this negative feeling, than the brain will reinforce and amplify your feelings of unhappiness. The more you notice the worst, or interpret events in a negative way, the more your brain will simply follow your direction and strengthen these negative pathways. People can get to such a low level that even things that should cheer them up find a connection to these strong 'unhappy' neural pathways. How many times have you tried to cheer someone up only to make him or her even more depressed? You may have done this yourself. The truth of the matter is that you get the brain you create by what you notice and your attitude while you are noticing.

This explains the reason behind sayings like, 'think happy thoughts' and 'look on the bright side'. This process, plus the fascinating new understanding of 'mirror neurons' (Section 3 – Hardwired to Connect) and the concept that humans prefer to move toward a state of harmony (Section 2) finally allows us to know the processes behind 'smile and the world smiles with you'.

Self-esteem is the great battle waged against us by the winner/loser world. Low self-esteem is primarily a winner/loser world creation and most of the distress caused by low self-esteem can simply disappear in the creative world. That is not to say, however, that our self-esteem doesn't rise and fall. It certainly does, but in the creative world these ups and downs act as information to help us understand how our emotional needs are being affected. These natural fluctuations are information and messages that enhance the experience.

Our esteem level can act as an indicator of whether an outcome is desirable or undesirable. In the creative world 'esteem' is not about whether you are worthy as a person, but whether you feel worthy *in that experience*. If you are becoming involved in something and you begin to feel that it is just 'not right' then it is our sense of self-esteem that shows us whether this is an experience in which you are pleased and proud to participate or not. In the winner/loser world the justification for participating in something that makes you feel bad about yourself is that the end result makes you a winner. More often than not, even if you do become a winner, you feel so bad about it that there is no pleasure at all. Cheating is one of those things. You might win, but at what personal cost?

So, self-esteem is a natural feeling within you that sends you a message. You are able to gauge whether this experience is right for you. This feeling is healthy and beneficial and only gets us into trouble when we believe that winning is the important goal. We know this is not true. Living a harmonious life is the important goal. Wise people have been telling us this for centuries, but we don't really need a wise person to tell us what we already know. To live a life that is an expression of our potential we must listen to the messages of happiness, inspiration and self-esteem that tell us we are treading the path that is true for us.

◆◆◆ ANGER AND ROAD RAGE ◆◆◆

THOUGHT: *Anger is such a winner/loser world issue. Road rage must be a about this type of anger.*

We hear so much discussion about the horrors of road rage and the terrible damage that anger creates in our society, but very little about what anger is, where it comes from and why it exists at all. The first thing to do with any situation is to ask a million questions. There are a number of very useful techniques to help mollify anger and reduce its intensity. I will repeat these later, but for now it may be better to think about where anger comes from and whether it is possible for it not to arise in the first place.

Anger can be reduced to two principal reasons: it is a result of frustration; and it is a mechanism to intimidate or frighten off. Anger is a natural and beneficial behaviour that has helped us survive. When a situation is getting desperate the body will shift into a state of anger in order to survive. If you are fighting the saber-tooth tiger and you realise you are going to lose your body will shift into a different level. Caution is suspended and fear is lost in an act of desperation. Anger produces one final uncontrolled burst of fight in order to defeat an assailant.

It is often described as 'behaving like a wild animal' and to a large extent this is true. We tap into parts of our brain that have been successfully inhibited by the cortex. In a fit of anger there is no thinking, no reason and no control. That is why it is so frightening in a world that doesn't have saber-toothed tigers and only threatens us with 30-year mortgages and unachievable sales targets. That is also why it is such an effective weapon to use against a perceived threat. As long as the other person doesn't retaliate then an angry person can tend to get what they want. Consequently, the threat of anger is often used against people that are unlikely to retaliate. This, all too often, is women, children and the less aggressive or more inhibited.

Road rage can seem to be a safe thing to do because you are protected behind the metal and glass of the vehicle. The other person is also constrained by their vehicle and the flow of traffic or other road rules. So, if this anger is not to intimidate or win or threaten, what is the point? Here we see the effect of frustration on our behaviour.

Frustration is the inability to achieve what you consider to be a necessary goal. If you are a bit hungry, then you don't really mind if the hamburger shop you pass is closed. As your hunger grows and each shop you pass is also closed you begin to feel frustrated. When you finally realize that it is a public holiday and all the food shops are closed your frustration increases and you begin to feel desperate. You become completely focused on the task of finding food. The more shops you find closed the more desperate you become until, at some point, you lose control, throw caution to the wind and find yourself bashing a vending machine with a crowbar in order to feed on the chocolate bars and chips inside. When the police arrive to arrest you there is a struggle as you resist this new frustrating restriction of people stopping you getting your chocolate bar. In the fight your pocket is ripped and a quantity of coins is strewn across the footpath. You stop, aghast, because there are plenty of coins to have legally and peacefully paid for the chocolate and chips. That's the real danger of anger – you abandon your capacity to think. For any person who might be the object of your anger, this is a very scary situation.

Once you are in a state of anger it is probably too late to stop the damage. People describe anger as feeling like "I completely lost it", "I didn't know what I was doing". Many can't even remember what happened because the hippocampus had completely shut down, discontinuing the process of remembering. The time to deal with anger is before it starts.

The winner/loser world is a hotbed of frustration. When the world you live in demands that you win and then makes it almost impossible to do so, it produces a persistent frustration. When the stress levels of work have left you in a state of 'tight and ready', the body is literally looking for something to fight or flee from in order to satisfy the biological messages. Driving a car in heavy traffic, especially on a hot day or when the car is stuffy, is simply a straw that would break anyone's back. Add to that the not unreasonable concern that your life is under threat when someone does something stupid on the road near you. The real surprise is that there is not more road rage. Perhaps we should take some heart from the amount of control and constraint that people exhibit even in the face of very dangerous or risky behaviour.

I remember a time when I was in fairly heavy traffic on a three-lane highway. Traffic was moving slowly, but reasonably smoothly. There was nowhere to rush to so I left a safe gap of a few car lengths between me and the car in front. As I drove along I realized that the car behind me was coming very close, then falling back and coming up close again. Clearly he wanted me to go faster, to close the gap. There was absolutely nothing to be gained so I maintained my 'safety gap'. After a few minutes the car behind veered into the middle lane causing another driver to brake, drove just ahead of me and then pulled back into my lane causing me to brake. He then proceeded to drive in front of me, up very close to the bumper bar of the car in front for the next 15 minutes because the traffic was too heavy to get any further. He just couldn't seem to *bear* the idea that there was space in front of me. Somehow I was making him a loser by denying him the ability to be 10 metres further forward. I suspect that he actually felt good about beating me and gaining those extra 10 metres. Crazy, but in the context of the winner/loser world, just another predictable outcome. When gaining 10 metres in heavy traffic allows someone to feel better and a winner, then the frustration and disappointment he experiences in his life must be awful. Sad really, but it would have been a lot sadder and lot more dangerous if I had decided to 'defend' my 10 metres of territory!

Anger can be cut off before it occurs by using *the problem is a message*. If I find myself beginning to get angry I stop and consider what is frustrating me. When someone is using anger to intimidate, look not so much at what they are trying to win, but what they are afraid of losing. Quite often people are afraid of losing their pride or superiority or having to admit something that may open them to criticism. Anger warrants concern, pity and help. What happens all too often is that anger is responded to with constraint, criticism or more anger. Situations escalate out of control very quickly and very easily.

When someone is out of control it is quite useless to yell at them to "get control of yourself!" By that stage it is probably too late. Leaving the scene, if possible, is a good idea. Remaining calm and attentive is another strategy that can help. Distraction is one of the best strategies because the mind is not dead, just not very logical or sensible. This is often what we do with a child having a tantrum. Adults can also respond to distraction. The trick is not to let anger get away. At the first signs, hear the message that something needs to be done. At this stage, when there is still control, it can be beneficial to show care and understanding and even affection. Difficult as this may be, it can have the opposite effect to escalation. As they said in the 1960s, "make love, not war".

◆◆◆ EXAM PRESSURE ◆◆◆

THOUGHT: *Young people are collapsing into stress as they study for and sit for major exams. It's as if an exam is a life and death issue. What can we do in the creative world to help?*

There are two major demons working here: expectation and right/wrong. There is also a fair smattering of guilt involved, and certainly a desire to avoid criticism. On top of that, exams, especially major ones at the end of high school, college and university, are held up as the be-all and end-all of the student's future. Worse still, in relation to employment opportunities, this may often be true. No wonder our young people are falling apart, giving up and dropping out.

School exams have become elements of a teenager's rite of passage. Many of our historic rituals have been lost as we change our focus to the power of money and the prestige of employment. James Hillman discusses this issue in *Tales of Power*. He describes the shift of what has been the dominating focus of power through history from religion to royalty to science, and now to money, prestige and influence. What makes you powerful can vary. At the moment it is money and associated elements like business and education.

There is a lot at stake when you sit for an exam. You are submitting yourself to a form of measurement, of quality assessment. If you 'measure up' then your progress will be easier and better rewarded. If you don't do well, get good marks, gain entry to higher education or secure a career opportunity, then your passage is much more difficult and much less rewarded. That is not to say that some people are not able to overcome these difficulties, but not everyone. A good result in an exam means you are rewarded – you're a winner; bad results and you are a loser. As we have seen in the book so far, being a winner or a loser has such a depth of implication and repercussion that it is no wonder there is so much fear about exams.

It is important to note that it is healthy to have a motivating dose of stress. Anything that stretches our skills and tests our development will evoke stress in the body. The biological reaction to stress enables systems that will improve our performance and enhance our utilization of our talents. Equally, we have seen what happens in the brain when there is excessive stress and when stress is prolonged into anxiety. The most important side effects are the shutting down of the learning mechanisms and the systems for memory recall.

I have heard parents say that stress is good for their children. They believe that it shows the children appreciate the importance of their exams. Many deliberately push their children to perform better, often by criticizing less than perfect results. One of the worst techniques used to motivate children is to withhold affection and to amplify disapproval. This leads children to believe that their school achievements are synonymous with their value as a person and their value as a member of the family. It is certainly true that social structures are tied to school results. Most employers want to hire the brightest people. Schools are graded on the performance of their students. Private schools are able to charge higher fees, which parents pay in the hope that the prestige of the school will make their child more successful. It is no wonder that many students who are bright and highly capable are often the students who suffer from this form of performance stress.

So, what can we do about it? The first question is, "What are we trying to win?" Then comes, "What are we afraid of losing?" Then the magic question: "What can we create?" Joseph Campbell suggests that we are born with potential, and that our life experience is to discover and manifest that potential. To this end he believed that you *could* simply follow your bliss, or follow what it is that you do best, in order to achieve that goal. This idea is echoed in many other sources.

The difficulty is that our social needs have become institutionalized and generalized. Just as no-one can ever be a social stereotype, neither can someone comply with a socially rigid education program. As it stands now, everyone has to learn the same information and sit for the same exams in order to prepare themselves for the same jobs. It is entirely possible for someone to never question anything, learn what they are taught, apply this in the way they are asked and work their whole life without making any particular contribution. They may even get a gold watch at retirement. Sadly, this may be true for more people than we would like to think. That is another reason why we are going crazy. It is not only those who are falling apart, but also those that have never been able to discover or express their potential even though they have done everything the winner/loser world has demanded.

Education needs to be about the availability of information and the opportunity to utilize this information to integrate our unique potential into a harmonious outcome and an enjoyable life. To do this we must be able to engage in the process, not just be dragged along by it. When you look at the education system, the people involved, the institutions, the needs of society, the needs of the economy and a host of other issues, you can see how hard it is for education to be an inspiring experience. Mostly it is an instructional experience. It is also a constant environment of success and failure. Success and failure become the pervading elements of the student's experience. The student is trapped in a winner/loser world.

There are numerous people who know that education can be so much more than just filling kids' heads with exam material. One of the most accessible places for school instruction to be transformed into inspiring information is at the family dinner table or lounge room. This is a wonderful environment for discussion and investigation. The sharing of ideas, the sharing of knowledge, the development of philosophies and the comparison of generational views are just a few of the outcomes of engagement within families. The dining-room table is readily available to many, but this venue often lies silent and unused. Television can nullify conversation and separate eating into rooms with their own TVs and computers. This can act to disconnect families even when they are living in the same house.

Exam stress is not about the thrill of learning, but the disproportionate imperative to be a successful winner. What can we create with the interaction of knowledge and our potential? The god of money and economics must be balanced with the greater need for engagement in our life experience and improvement of the human connection.

♦♦♦ PEER PRESSURE ♦♦♦

THOUGHT: *Doing the right thing by other people when I was at school led me into a lot of behaviour that I wish hadn't happened. I learnt, but it hurt a lot on the way.*

Peer pressure is the way in which other people try to get you to do what they want. The interesting question is, what do other people think they want? One of the basic criticisms that is used to pressure someone into doing what the group wants is to make them feel as though they are not good enough or that there must be something wrong with them. This is very effective, particularly if they are young. Peer pressure is not, however, restricted to young people at school.

There are pressures at work. Workmates who like to socialize after work can make you feel very uncomfortable about preferring to go home to family or friends. Even more difficult is the pressure to work overtime. I can remember when I worked in an office environment the work contract involved unpaid overtime when required. My day officially ended at 5.30pm. As I packed up to leave I noticed that the other men on the sales staff would just hang around. There didn't even seem to be anything for them to do, but they stayed in the office. I'm sure the owner of the business liked to see workers who stayed longer in the office. I'm also sure that is why these men stayed. I must admit that I didn't last long in that job.

I am not advocating that you shouldn't work hard or do extra hours at work if that leads to a productive, creative outcome for you. I'm referring to the *pressure* we feel to comply. The pressure is amplified when we feel that we are not as good or as dedicated because we don't comply. This type of peer pressure is a plague in our work environment. I have even seen it in voluntary work environments. It is also interesting that much of this pressure is unspoken. You are just *supposed* to do it. And we do.

The simplest underlying pressure in most advertising is to tell you that you are not good enough – until you buy the product and solve your insufficiency. I've often wondered how washing could be 'whiter than white'. Products often achieve the impossible. There is an almost spiritual message in some advertising. How is it possible to feel like you are in heaven by using a particular cheese spread? One of the most blatant advertisements in this vein was on a billboard. The ad was for shoes, and the slogan entreated 'Our shoes have soul'. What on earth do they mean by that? Interestingly, I suspect that if that was an ad in the 1980's it would have been the pun, 'Our shoes have sole'. This ad actually gives us a lot of information about our social feelings. If people are interested in buying shoes with 'soul', then the advertisers believe that people feel they are in need of soul. The dreadful irony is that it is the winner/loser world that is causing us to feel like we are losing our soul in the first place. People have actually said to me that they feel that the competitive world has cost them their soul. So, the winner/loser world robs people of their soul and then sells them a substitute inside a pair of shoes. Now that has to be considered good marketing! It may drive people crazy, but is great for the financial bottom-line (pardon my cynicism).

But we digress. To get back to the main discussion, human beings don't like to feel alone or isolated. The best thing to do is to open up to others and allow them to engage in your experience and you in theirs. The difficulty is that if you are in the winner/loser world, like the people in *The Matrix*, then you often don't *know* you are in a winner/loser world. A way to feel connected with others in the winner/loser world is to get people to do what you are doing. If you can pressure people into doing what you want, then you can get a feeling of not being alone. You also maintain your winning ways and may even amplify your winning position. Wow! Who could resist that? Well, what happens when it doesn't work? What happens when your group is usurped by another group? The pressure to be a part of the 'in crowd' becomes an unending battle. Just when you thought you had everyone with you they desert for something else.

That sounds a bit crazy when you read it, but that's what happens. In the winner/loser world these results are not just unfortunate errors, they are predictable results. That is why the winner/loser world has to be recognized and understood, otherwise these things are going to continue to manifest.

It is important to note here that the creative process occurs *whenever* elements interact – even in the winner/loser world. *What* we create is a reflection of the elements that we include in our interactions and the degree of energy each element is given. If you allow the winner/loser world to be a dominating energy, then predominantly, winner/loser world results will be created. This is why helping people back from their troubles, but putting them back into the winner/loser world, will just result in another winner/loser situation being created, eventually. If you help someone out of the water, just to throw them back in again, means they will never get dry.

✦✦✦ **CREATIVE INTELLIGENCE** ✦✦✦

THOUGHT: *How are we able to do all these things? What if people don't understand some of it? How can we be creative when everyone else is winner/loser? How do we control it?*

The term, creative intelligence, has been used in recent years, but often as a buzzword or a type of shorthand or generic name for something more general. With a quick web search it is easy to find a number of interesting web pages on creative intelligence. Tony Buzan, who developed Mind Mapping, discusses this in his book on Creative Intelligence by showing how to 'tap into your creative genius'. Maharishi Mahesh Yogi has looked at the relationship of Creative Intelligence and Vedic knowledge utilising the process of Transcendental Meditation. There are countless advertising and corporate people using the term. I was interested in The Centre for Creative Intelligence run by Mary Taylor who looks at creativity in the individual from the psychotherapeutic point of view. Her catchphrase is "to see yourself and your abilities clearly".

All these people are making valuable contributions. Mostly their focus is on our outward creative expression and the ways in which we can improve ourselves and understand ourselves better. I suggest that these works are helpful in the battle against the winner/loser world, but are still aiming at making us winners or, at least, better 'swimmers'. However, I believe it is now possible to define this term, creative intelligence, to a deeper, more elemental level.

As we have discussed so far, creativity is not only outward expressions like art or music. Creativity is what happens *whenever* elements interact. It is a name we give to the process that naturally and inevitable occurs during integration – as things mix together.

To say there is 'intelligence' means that there is some form of purposeful goal based on some type of intention. If creativity is a purely random act with no degree of preferential outcome, then nothing would matter and everything would be acceptable. We know this is not so.

We are more familiar with IQ (intelligence quotient) at school. This problem solving intelligence is defined as our 'ability to acquire and apply information towards a purposeful goal'. Although we mostly look on this as a process of conscious thought, there is a lot more to it. Have you ever had trouble finding the answer to something and decided to 'sleep on it'? When you wake the answer is miraculously in your mind. There is not a lot of conscious thinking going on during sleep, but we are discovering that there is certainly a creative process continuing in the brain even when you sleep. Elements are always interacting. Our conscious awareness is the state of mind where we can *know* and consider what our brain is processing, but our brain processing all the time. Conscious awareness is just one level.

Our creative intelligence quotient, let's call it CIQ, is observable in the natural reactions we have when we are or are not integrating towards a harmonious outcome. We know from neuroscience that our brain prefers to be in a state of F.A.C.E.S. (flexible, active, coherent, energetic and stable). We can readily observe that our emotions and feelings prefer to be in a state of H.A.R.M.O.N.Y. (happy, able, receptive, mindful, open, nascent and yes). We also know from complexity theory that when things interact (the simple state) they will seek to integrate to a more complex state as a natural and necessary event. This means that the creative process is more than just a name for some random, uncontrolled process. Creativity is a process towards a preferred outcome: toward a state of harmony.

The body, mind and soul are not satisfied or content until a state of harmony is achieved. If there is not a state of harmony then aspects of the body, mind and soul will send clear messages through our health, our emotions and our sensitivity that more needs to be done.

An interesting side effect from this is a feeling of 'other self'. Because we continue to seek a harmonious outcome even when we are not consciously aware of it (in fact, not thinking can often help), our lives can sometimes feel as if some unknown force is driving them. We might feel as if we are being guided to places, people and situations independent of our personal intervention or participation. It can feel as though it 'just happened'. The reality is, more simply, that our 'creative intelligence' has continued to act regardless of our conscious participation.

Despite our boneheaded perception that 'nothing is happening' just because we are not thinking about it, we are in a constant process of interaction. Every moment involves interaction between our environment and our thoughts, feelings, needs, desires, wants, hopes and wishes. *Everything* is *always* changing and there is an 'intelligent' preference toward a harmonious change. This occurs even if we are too overpowered by the winner/loser world, to notice.

Creative Intelligence (CIQ) is a good term to describe the mechanisms you use when you are in the creative world and living the creative world way. To answer the question, "How do I *do* this creative world thing?" earns the response, "With your creative intelligence". When you creatively participate in your experience of life you can trust your CIQ to find a harmonious outcome.

Your IQ will solve intellectual problems when you acquire the necessary information. Your CIQ will find a harmonious outcome when you creatively participate. It is necessary for us to connect, to engage and to be response-able. The winner/loser world blocks these necessities through disconnection and disengagement.

The ability to solve problems with IQ is natural and irresistible. The ability to solve problems well and to solve increasingly complex problems is dependent on the acquisition of knowledge. That is why we benefit from education and sharing experience. Someone with a high IQ can still do stupid things without the necessary knowledge.

Our creative intelligence, CIQ, is also natural and irresistible. To achieve a harmonious outcome is dependent on being *connected* and *engaged* with people, things, actions and reactions – the whole environment.

Our CIQ tells us that we are not in harmony through the messages of the 7 Demons and the 8 Differences of the winner/loser world. We must listen to these messages and see how the winner/loser world is restricting what we include in our lives and what we notice in our environment. Joseph Campbell urged us to 'follow our bliss'. Now we can do so with confidence, knowing that our faith in ourselves is supported by an inner 'intelligence'. We *will* end up somewhere better in the creative world.

◆ ◆ ◆ ◆ ◆ ◆ ◆ ◆ ◆ ◆ ◆

Section 2 must come to a close, even though there is much more that can be said. I'm sure you have thought of a host of topics that you believe could be discussed. Discovering the new freedoms of the creative world is an ongoing project. There will never be a final result, only an endless stream of outcomes.

That just leaves me to explain why there is a Section 3. Section 3 is titled *For the Geeks* because it is speculative, a bit technical and, hopefully, a bit 'out there'. I encourage you to read on and see what you think. But firstly, the second parable.

● THE PARABLE OF THE DUCK ●

Every year Harold, the duck, flew south for the winter. This year he was sick of it. Maybe it was his mid-life crisis. He was, after all, nearly seven. So, this year, Harold wasn't flying anywhere.

All his friends and family tried to talk him out of it, but eventually everyone left and Harold stood defiantly on his own. Winter began to close in and Harold learnt something new. Winter is very cold. He began to shiver and no amount of fluffing his feathers helped. Eventually he realised that flying south may have been a good idea after all. Better late than never and off he flew.

But it was even colder up in the sky. Ice began to form on his wings and it was harder and harder to flap until finally he could flap no more. He did his best to glide down to land. His wings were frozen and he figured that this was the end. He was a dead duck. To be killed in a crash landing is very rare and very embarrassing. Harold saw a field below with heavy grass so he aimed for the grassiest spot. It was a bit rough, but he survived. It was very exhilarating.

As he lay there, trying to get his breath, Harold saw a cow wandering towards him. Now he wondered if he was going to be killed under the hooves of the cow. He'd never heard of a duck dying like that. To his amazement the cow stopped right over the top of Harold. He opened one of his eyes that had been squeezed shut in anticipation of being squashed and he looked up just in time to see the cow lift its tail. The cow was about to release a cowpat right on top of Harold. His wings were still frozen so there was no way to escape. What duck had ever been killed by a cowpat? This was just terrible.

The cowpat splattered all over Harold, but instead of killing him, Harold began to feel warm. He was able to move his wings. He could stand up, but now the sticky, grassy mess of the cowpat was holding him down. It dawned on Harold that he might drown in this horrible cowpat. He was not having a good day.

Out of the corner of his eye Harold saw a tabby cat strolling through the grass. What if the cat could pull him out of this stinking cowpat? With a bit of help Harold could see that he might survive this whole disaster of a day. He stood up as best he could and flapped his wings as much as they would in the sticky mess. The cat looked over in his direction. It stopped and stared. Harold moved up and down and flapped like crazy. The cat began to come toward Harold so he kept flapping. The cat seemed to get quite excited and bounded over the tufted grass toward Harold who began to truly believe he would be saved.

As quick as you like the cat pulled Harold from the cowpat and shook him a few times to get rid of the excess cow dung from his feathers. Then, just as quick as he pleased, the cat ate Harold in a couple of mouthfuls.

◆ ◆ ◆ ◆ ◆ ◆ ◆ ◆ ◆ ◆

The moral of this story? Not everything that craps on you is bad and not everything that pulls you out of the crap is good. Indeed, every situation creates interactions and every interaction creates change, although not always the one you expect or the one you plan.

SECTION 3

FOR THE GEEKS

CONTENTS

♦♦♦ FOR THE GEEKS ♦♦♦

What is our fascination with the mysterious? Perhaps the winner/loser world lets us down so often it is more satisfying to connect with the inexplicable, the undefinable and the unquestionable. They can never let you down because they have no positive existence or interactive reality. You can't create with them. They are benign.

This final section holds some of the fascinating pieces of information that I have come across along the journey. These ideas, suggestions and speculations are here to titillate your thinking processes and tease you with what we know, what we nearly know and what is possible to know. Some of the research presented here is very new. I have also made some personal speculations and discuss possible implications in order to spark your interest, personal assessment and, hopefully, your imagination. On another level, I want to show you some of the intellectual foundation to the winner/loser world theory that didn't quite fit into Section 1 or 2. There is great deal more that I simply have no room for. I encourage you to delve into the recommended reading list.

The great scientist, Louis Pasteur said, 'fortune favours the prepared mind'. If you'll pardon my paraphrasing: It's amazing what you stumble across when you know stuff.

I hope that this section prepares you for greater fortune or, at least, inspired stumbling.

♦♦♦ PLATO'S ALLEGORY OF THE CAVE ♦♦♦

It must be very flattering to think that you have thought of something completely new. It must have been amazing for the likes of Charles Darwin, Albert Einstein and Stephen Hawking to realise that they were thinking something that had never been thought of before. When I first looked around the current literature for something similar to the winner/loser world idea I couldn't find anything quite like it. Then I saw *The Matrix,* which strongly reflected the unreal 'real world' scenario. The Wachowski brothers never claimed to be more than a couple of guys presenting some interesting philosophy. So, where did they get the idea? I had to go back quite a long way.

Plato described the idea of a separate, limiting style of living some 2,400 years ago. Talk about my idea not being new! Sometime around 360-390 BC Plato wrote his famous work, *The Republic,* which contained a description called *The Allegory of the Cave.* This was used to illustrate his Theory of Forms. I'll describe it briefly here, but you might like to look it up for greater detail.

The scene is set in a cave where prisoners are chained into a position that forces them to look at the wall of a cave. These 'mental prisoners' are *unable* to be aware of anything other than what they see on the cave wall. Behind them burns a fire. Between the fire and the prisoners there is a parapet. Along this parapet are puppeteers who act out the experiences of life using the real objects of life. The prisoners, however, can only see the shadow dance on the wall of the cave that the puppeteers create. The prisoners believe that the images they see are the true events of life, but they are only looking at a shadowy representation of what is really happening behind them. They have no way of appreciating or understanding the true nature of the objects. Here is an illustration of Plato's Cave:

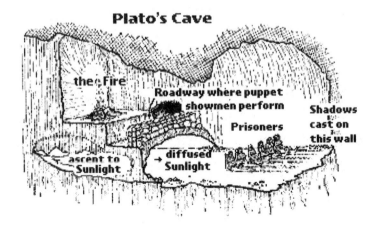

Plato's Cave

the Fire

Roadway where puppet
showmen perform

Shadows
cast on
this wall

Prisoners

ascent to
Sunlight

diffused
Sunlight

The prisoners take appearance for reality without any knowledge of the real causes of the shadows. So when the prisoners talk about what they see it is only about what the shadow is doing and what it looks like, but not what the object or action really is and what it represents. They are not able to interact with the experience themselves, just watch with uninvolved objectivity and/or a subjective participation that has no control or influence.

There is lot more interesting material in relation to the Forms, but that is all that is relevant for our purposes. The cave wall represents what we are able to experience in the winner/loser world. There is no capacity to be truly involved, to creatively participate or positively influence the situation. The 'prisoners' are constrained in a separated condition even though they may be sitting together. The puppeteers are the manipulators, of both people and social structures. They decide what experiences we are able to witness.

To break free of the chains the prisoners need to firstly become curious and questioning about the nature of what they are looking at. The Catch-22 is that they don't know that what they are seeing is anything but the truth. They have no awareness to inspire questioning. Socrates, another great philosopher of this time, encouraged us to question and to critically evaluate even what may seem obvious. It seems that the winner/loser world was already entrenched way back then. It is through questioning that the prisoners can discover their plight.

Rather than talking about what they see in the assumption that it is true, the prisoners need to talk about their experience as an investigation of what other meaning it could have. They can even question what they believe to be true. They need to take a *that's interesting* approach! This will invoke interaction and interaction will enable the creative process to alter their mental perspective. When the prisoners begin to really look at each other they will eventually realize they are wearing chains and wonder what they are for. With some co-operation it may be possible to remove the chains from each other. These are all creative world outcomes that will soon lead to freedom from the chains and the realization that the shadow play is not the 'real world' after all.

The idea of people living in a constructed 'world' that is intended to manipulate and control is also seen in other books. George Orwell wrote *1984* about a society where history and truth were created every day in order to suit Big Brother. Aldous Huxley devised an apparent utopia in *Brave New World*, but this came at the expense of family, religion, culture and creativity. The correct word for this is *dystopia*, which is, essentially, the opposite of utopia. You might describe it as a *dysfunctional utopia* where all appears well until you scratch the surface and find the truth. Our modern, winner/loser world might well look like a potential utopia, but we don't even have to scratch the surface to see that this is not true. The evidence is coming from the epidemic of unhappiness, which is our natural indicator (CIQ) that we are not integrating in a harmonious direction. Now that I am conscious of the winner/loser world and have a semantic description to reflect upon, it seems so obvious. I sometimes wonder why it took me so long to figure it out.

◆◆◆ IS SYMBOLISM AN INSTINCT? ◆◆◆

It seems that symbolic thinking is not inherent in the brain at birth, but rather an outcome of the developing mind. Dr Judy DeLoache, at the University of Virginia, has found that it is not until a child is around three-years-old that they grasp the idea of dual representation. Until the mind can see an object as both itself and as representing something else, the mind is unable to think symbolically. If shown a miniature model of a room where a sweet is hidden, then taken to a life size room that is exactly the same, the sub three-year-old is not able to see that the rooms are the same and will not look for the sweet. A post three-year-old will quickly discover the sweet and gobble it up.

The human brain is not fully developed at birth and will almost double in size during childhood. It is believed that the brain continues to develop right into our early 20s. Some areas of the brain will continue to create new neurons (neurogenesis) throughout life. We know this happens in the dentate gyrus within the hippocampus as a part of the process of learning. Now we are beginning to see that neurogenesis is possible in other parts of the brain through the process of activating stem cells that exist in the brain tissue.

Just recently there has been work that discovered a very important difference in the human brain compared to other primates: human brains will establish a greater network of connection and integration. This means that more parts of our brain can interact and this multiplies what can be achieved by brain activity. Dr Daniel Siegel calls his work Interpersonal Neurobiology, as he investigates the nature of not only the integration of the brain within itself, but how there is a connection between brains and minds of more than one person. Dr Ernest Rossi has done extraordinary work in understanding the way the brain's activity motivates and activates gene expression and the process of creating new synaptic connections and new neurons. These are two people whose work I suggest you investigate.

But, back to symbolism. You may know people that you might describe as being 'literalists'. They tend to think about things in a direct and obvious way. This may seem to be limiting. These people can sometimes find jokes difficult because they don't perceive the double meaning or recognize the comedic twist. This literalist approach can also be when the discussion is close to regular day-to-day activities. An interesting result was recorded in an IQ test that examined both city and country boys. A mathematical question that went something like, 'If there are six sheep in one enclosure and there are eight enclosures on an acre of land, then what is the area of each enclosure and how many sheep can be held?' The city boys all presented an answer, but a number of the country boys were confused. When asked, their response was, 'You wouldn't have that many sheep in an enclosure that small.' The boys were looking at the literal image and not the idea that it represented. This indicates that the brain acts in relation to what is being noticed. The city boys thought about the question as a calculation, the country boys thought about the question in relation to their day-to-day experience. This has important implications regarding our point of view when we consider the world around us.

We now know that not only what we take notice of, but also the attitude we bring to bear while we are noticing, will affect which part of the brain responds. The parts of the brain that respond are the ones that will be reinforced into strong neural pathways and are also the areas that can develop new synaptic connections (to learn). This means that if you see something that is horrible and you feel horrible about it, then you will activate the areas of your brain that support these feelings. The brain will respond with neurotransmitters and other chemicals that generally respond to such feelings. If you have a stressful attitude, you will activate stress-based neural pathways and release stress-based chemicals. If, on the other hand, you see something that may be horrible, but with an attitude that does not promote a horrible feeling, then the brain will act accordingly and different chemicals will be released. In short, if you have a happy, positive disposition you will be happier than if you have a sad, negative disposition. Negative thoughts will activate the negative parts of the brain and that will influence what you notice. It may even feel that you have drawn negative things toward you. Attracting negativity has been a catchphrase in the self-development talk for some years and this may go some way to explaining how that happens.

It is difficult, however, to be bright and happy about some of the horrible things that go on in this world. The issue is, though, not what is happening, but the nature of your disposition. Let me use the example of Mother Teresa. I heard this story from the extraordinary Jean Houston. When Mother Teresa was asked how she was able to see such horror and stay so peaceful, she responded with words similar to: "I am truly married to my beloved Jesus and He is in everything I see and do. When I look at these things I do not see the horror, but I see my Beloved, who is in us all. There is nothing that I cannot or will not do for my Beloved and that is why I do not see the horror, only love."

We all do that to some extent. Parents are well known for seeing their children this way. This is a very empowering capacity. If you do not have a fearful and stressful disposition to win then everything you respond to will *not* include those negative points-of-view that the winner/loser world enables. The stress of not being successful or having a bad result or feeling guilty or being wrong will not *exist* in your brain. You will not be drawn to notice those things as a negative part of your experience and, possibly, you may either not attract or even repel those negative elements in your environment. Instead of seeing and experiencing these horrors every day, you will only see love – an uninhibited creative interaction. Now that is interesting.

♦♦♦ TIME AS AN EXPRESSION OF COMPLEXITY ♦♦♦

It may seem an odd question, but why does time move forward? We know that time moves in a particular direction, because if we look at a film running backwards we know that it is, indeed, running backwards. There are some that say time is just a figment of our psychology and that is related to the linear nature of our perception. What contributes to that perception?

From the cosmological point of view the direction of time has two essential elements. The first is that things began in a state of low entropy. (Entropy simply means disorder. Low entropy is more ordered, or less complex, than high entropy, which is the same as saying that high entropy is more disordered or complex.) The second is that there is a process of mixing. When two things mix, they produce something that is more complex. So, in relation to the original elements we now have something that is in a higher degree of disorder or complexity. Think of coffee and milk. The milk is in an ordered arrangement until you put it in the coffee and stir. The milk molecules interact with the coffee molecules and produce a more complex arrangement. This is also the essence of Complexity Theory in mathematics.

It is not possible for a cup of white coffee to exist before there is some black coffee and some milk. Equally it is only when these two elements come together and mix that there is a change. The question of how the elements of the universe might come together and mix inspired Vahe Guradyan of La Sapienza University in Rome to hypothesise that space was shaped with a negative curvature (like a Pringle chip, it seems) that enabled particles to encounter each other, interact and validate the concept of a universe that progresses into a state of higher entropy. So, what has this got to do with the winner/loser world?

Surprisingly, quite a lot. If the forward passage of time is marked by an increase in complexity because of the process of interaction (mixing), then this supports the idea that when elements interact they will seek to integrate (remember the chapter on Harmony). This cosmological idea adds weight, or at least relevance, to the idea that elements seek to integrate because that is the natural process of the passage of time.

We certainly can feel when nothing is happening that time is dragging by, but when you are busily interacting time hurries along. That is not to say that time is based on whether we are busy or not. What I am meaning is that we have a psychological perception of time that is linked to the process of changes from low to high entropy.

At this point, I freely accept that this may be a long bow to draw. The connection is purely speculative, but what is interesting is that the speculation occurs at all. Here is a vibrant example of the process of creativity: where there is interaction there is a creative process that is inclined toward a state of harmony. That just means that I am inclined to think thoughts that make me feel good. It makes me feel good to find flickers of interconnection with ideas that are from widely diverse origins and disciplines.

The conclusion is that it is reasonable to say that *my* ideas, when interacting with the article about the *Arrow of Time* in *New Scientist* magazine combine to create a new and more complex idea. In doing so, I have been able to *feel* the passage of time. That *feeling* enables me to know that I have gone from one moment to another - that I have become more. I am in a state of higher entropy and there is no returning to the previous lower entropy state. I may have been milk a few moments ago, but now I am white coffee. There is no possibility of becoming milk ever again. I can, of course, become something more than white coffee. In fact, as times moves forward (and I continue to interact) I have no option. I only have the option of how I feel about it. So I might as well feel good and seek to integrate in a harmonious direction.

♦♦♦ HARDWIRED TO CONNECT ♦♦♦

We actually get inside each other's heads. Not just with some visual imagery or imaginative memory, but literally in the firing of neurons in our brain. This is a fabulous discovery regarding the way that brains interact. The discovery was accidental, as so often happens. In the 1980s and 1990s, Giacomo Rizzolatti was working with Leonardo Fogassi and Vittorio Gallese at the university in Parma, Italy. They were studying neurons that were specialized in the control of hand functions, like picking things up, grabbing things etc. An electrode was placed in the inferior frontal cortex of a monkey. During each experiment, they recorded responses from a single neuron in the monkey's brain while the monkey was allowed to reach for pieces of food.

At one point during a break in testing one of the researchers reached for a banana in the bowl. The monkey was still wired up and to everyone's amazement, the monkey's neuron fired even though he made no movement at all. This work has since been published and confirmed, with mirror neurons found in both inferior frontal and inferior parietal regions of the brain. It has also been shown to occur in humans.

Further work done by Marco Iacoboni shows that mirror neurons in humans will act when the movement has purposeful intention. If you move your hand to your mouth the observer has no mirror response, but if you hold a glass of water and raise that to your lips there will be a mirror neuron response. This has enormous implications in the nature of the way that empathy works. It is also related to the way in which we can imagine what people are about to do. It may even have some relevance to the process of clairvoyance and future prediction.

All these things are concerned with what happens after the mirror neuron event. Dr Daniel Siegel gives a great description:

> Mirror neurons allow us actually to take in the state of someone else and re-create it in our own bodies and our own emotional circuits in our brains. The next step after that compassionate resonance is to ... look with a different part of our brain ... the very front part right behind your eyes and you use that to actually notice what your body is feeling, make an interpretation of that ... and then you attribute that feeling in yourself to someone else and that ... is the way we are beginning to understand ... empathy.

We may not only be firing neural circuits that are the same as those in the brain of the person in front of us, but also we may then process that experience as if it were our own. If we are people of like mind or of similar experiences it shows that it is quite possible to really feel yourself to be in their shoes - not only in the present, but also the predictable future. Very interesting. I wonder what we can create with that idea?

◆◆◆ THE ENERGY EQUATION ◆◆◆

In the chapter on how creative experience can have an increase in energy (Section 2) I described the way that this may be possible. I have devised a mathematical formula that may have been too much of a distraction to include in Section 2. I am hoping this formula may prompt discussion and inspire other representations of the energy question.

As a reminder: when elements interact they will seek to integrate through the process of creativity resulting in a new outcome. Each element involved in the interaction possesses energy. If the creative process is uninhibited the energy in the outcome will be a combination of the energy of the initial elements. If there is any resistance there will be a diminishment in the collective energy potential. Resistance comes when the interaction encounters blockages or barriers. These blockages and barriers may be physical and/or emotional and/or rational. The ideal, resistance-free state is *unconditional positive regard*.

As a formula the process appears like this:

The amount of energy that is lost because of the resistance (z) indicates the severity and/or effectiveness of the inhibition. There will probably always be some degree of resistance, but if the process results in a higher level of energy in the new outcome, then the participant will feel more energetic.

In Dr Daniel Siegel's acronym of F.A.C.E.S. relating to harmony, this formula gives some explanation as to how there is an energetic element (E). The main issue here is that it is pleasurable to feel more energy during experiences. We tend to continue to do things that bring us pleasure.

Our system is designed to prefer an increase in energy levels and to improve the quality of our conscious experience when we seek an uninhibited and positive journey. Equally, when we begin an inhibited journey there will be reductions in energy, which enact chemical processes that make us feel tired, lethargic and depressed. During creative activity there is a set of systems in our brain that work to maximise positive pleasure and energy. The feelings come from:

1. positive anticipation – the neuro-transmitter, dopamine, is often described as the pleasure chemical in the brain. This is not quite accurate. It is more accurate to say that dopamine is active in the process of the pleasure we feel with positive anticipation. Dopamine is more about what is *going* to happen than what *is* happening. When there is positive anticipation we also utilise norepinephrine (noradrenalin), which is present in the generation of alertness and arousal: we feel more energised. When there is a satisfying fulfilment of the anticipation there are a number of mood enhancements, which include the involvement of serotonin. Disappointment and dissatisfaction are responses that can reduce the amount of serotonin involved and even release stress-related cortisols. Reduction in the availability of serotonin is one of the conditions of depression. In the creative world there are fewer possibilities for an outcome to be dissatisfying, and therefore there is less occurrence of lower serotonin.

2. no engagement of fear systems – when there is no fear of losing or failing or a bad result, there is less stress. Stress is an energetic resistance that reacts to changes the body enacts due to the secretion of stress-related chemicals. Cortisol will busily prepare the body for a perceived danger and, to do this, energy will be required. This will reduce the available energy in the outcome

3. open-ended outcome – this means that whatever the outcome there is a strong possibility of positively imagining the next step. This begins the cycle of positive anticipation again, which will increase the feeling of energy via dopamine and norepinephrine. The outcome becomes a new element in the next creative step.

4. reasonable moments of pause – letting outcomes have enough time to reach their potential or inspire a new step forward. When a result is quickly assessed and either accepted or rejected there is no opportunity for energy to be appreciated or encouraged. The

winner/loser world is a 'take-it-or-leave-it' place. The creative world is a 'take-it-and-make-something-more-of-it' place.

5. positive, integrated activity of the hippocampus – this creates an open mind to short-term memory and recall. Stress can reduce the effectiveness of the hippocampus and even close it down. When the hippocampus is active there is a direct connection to other parts of the cortex, especially the Prefrontal Cortex. This connection allows us to incorporate a myriad of additional elements into the interaction. Each of these elements adds a degree of 'energy' to the equation. This can and usually does occur outside of our conscious awareness. When people say 'I don't know where the energy comes from' they are quite correct. It is not within our direct control. What we put *into* the cortex as we learn from our experiences is the principle way in which we do have some control.

6. integration of the pre-frontal cortex and the limbic system – the process of all these areas of the brain is an integrated co-operation. As more of the brain becomes involved in activity, the more possibilities can arise. The big difference between human brains and other primates has been found to be that the human brain will form more and better connections and interactions. It is possible that the more of the brain you use the more the brain creates connections in order for more of the brain to be used. This only goes to reduce the inhibitions that occur when the brain prepares itself for fight-flight-freeze from prolonged stress or fear – whether real or imagined.

An energetic life is not:
1. adrenalin rush – this is just that pumped-up feeling and can be the sympathetic nervous system preparing for danger.
2. external motivation and stimulus – just because you are responding to energetic aspects in the environment

doesn't give lasting benefit. Usually when the external stimulus stops your energetic response stops as well.

3. aggression or assertiveness – again this is the fight system which is based around stress and largely closing down productive systems, particularly the hippocampus and interaction with the cortex.

4. power – being in a dominant position over others may feel like an energy burst, but it is based on aspects of egotism and fantasy. The biggest danger of basing your energy on power is that it is not long before others will try to take your power away and you have to defend your position. This takes you into stress and fear cycles that cost energy.

5. winning – this is similar to power, but is just the short-term buzz that comes from being better. Once the immediate event is passed the energy dissipates. The quick surge of energy at the moment of winning is also present in the creative world, but it is more about personal satisfaction than proving that you have value and worth.

These are all short term and energy spending processes that will eventually be unsustainable. To compensate for this people will supplement their systems with external stimulants like steroids, amphetamines and other chemical stimulants to force the body to feel energetic. This is a damaging punishment to the body and can have terrible side effects, even death.

The creative world promotes the sense that every act and all the elements in it are new and fresh because everything has changed in even the smallest moments of time. For example, when seeking an embrace from your loved one you are not embracing *again*, you are doing it for the first time for *that* moment. You are having a unique experience that has changed in some way from the last embrace. It has changed *because* of the last embrace. Anticipation of a pleasurable experience is regularly and persistently possible in the creative world, but highly problematic in the winner/loser world.

So, an important element of creativity is to allow the elements to interact without inhibition (on the assumption that the interaction will seek to find a harmonious outcome if all elements are allowed to fully express themselves). When elements interact they seek to integrate. The elements each have their own inherent energy contribution. The action of integration involves the process of creativity, which is affected by the presence of inhibition. Inhibition is a resistance and resistance expends energy so the end result is less energetic than the original elements. When creativity is uninhibited there is no resistance and so the energy of the individual elements compounds to produce an outcome whose energy is focussed and stronger than its parts. Simple really.

◆ DEPRESSION: WHAT HAPPENS IN YOUR BRAIN? ◆

Although counsellors and psychologists deal with emotional matters, it is surprising how few have a strong understanding about the mind and its physical expression, the brain. Dr Siegel has done a straw poll of audiences and has found that amongst tens of thousands of trained health professionals almost everyone has done a formal course in their training on mental illness, but only about 3-5% has had formal training in the mind or in mental health. It is no wonder that the average person has even less knowledge. There has, however, been an enormous amount of research into the brain over the last 20 years. George Bush Sr. proclaimed the 1990s as The Decade of the Brain, which was a valuable beginning, but what are we doing with the knowledge now?

In the September 2003 issue of *Scientific American*, Gary Stix proposed we call this time The Decade of Behaviour. I wonder if it might be better to spend this decade teaching, learning and integrating our new knowledge of the brain – a Decade of Information.

One of the discoveries that has truly altered our neuro-scientific approach to the brain is that it is more plastic, in more ways and for longer than was previously thought. Simplistically, this means that it is possible to learn, rearrange, replace and regrow neurons and synapses within the brain.

There are a host of important names that have risen into the limelight. Who would have thought that a neuroscientist could be 'cool'? Steven Pinker, one of the funniest writers of detailed information (*The Language Instinct, How the Mind Works*); Antonio Damasio (*Descartes Error, The Feeling of What Happens: Body and Emotion in the Making of Consciousness*), V.S. Ramachandran (*Phantom Limbs, A Brief Tour of Consciousness*); Daniel Dennett (*Kinds of Minds, Consciousness Explained*); Joseph LeDoux (*The Emotional Brain; Synaptic Self*); Susan Blackmore (*The Meme Machine; An Introduction to Consciousness*); and Susan Greenfield (The *Human Brain: A Guided Tour, Brain Story*) are great examples, and their popular publications have become best sellers. These, and many others, like Dr Daniel Siegel and Dr Ernest Rossi, are an irresistible source of information about the 'thing' that we are really dealing with when we are having trouble coping with life – the brain and the mind.

Much work has been done observing and studying the effects of selected lesions in animal brains and of human subjects who have suffered lesions from natural causes. It all started when Phineus Gage sent his gunpowder ramrod through his head and survived. Despite the fact that he had done irreparable damage to his pre-frontal cortex he did not seem to suffer any ill effects. He was a walking miracle. Over time, however, he changed. Gage suffered the demise of his personality and his better judgement. It was the first time we had seen the impact of damage to a specific part of the brain. Much has been learnt since then. Now we are seeing extraordinary discoveries.

Pioneers like Dr Amen have allowed us to actually see the brain alter during behaviour in patients with ADD; Dr Ramachandran has shown the neurological nature of phantom limbs in amputees; Joseph LeDoux has described the importance of chemical action between the synapses and how this relates to who we are and how we behave. We have begun to do more than just sit back and wonder at the mystery of the mind.

The discovery of neurotransmitters and the specific nature of their function have allowed for a clearer understanding of how our moods are regulated, modulated and how they get out of control. This, of course, has led to a raft of medications to 'normalise' brain chemical balance.

As I discussed earlier in relation to hunger, it is arguable that the body indicates its needs in a fairly clumsy fashion. Evolution has developed a system that is only required to improve our chances of survival. It is not required to make us perfect or super beings. The messages are not necessarily clear or particularly concise. These messages only enable us to take essential action. The simple human capacity to 'feel sick' requires a doctor to undergo years of study in order to be able to interpret the specific nature of the patient's 'sickness'.

We also produce a fairly clumsy indicator of emotional imbalance. We call this 'feeling depressed' or 'unhappy'. Trying to understand what this means in detail and how to help will continue to be an ongoing study for some time to come. There is a lot of material in psychological literature that acknowledges we have some innate sense of who we are or are best able to be. This is called the internal environment. The relationship between the needs of the internal environment and the external environment is indicated with feelings. If the relationship is harmonious then the feelings are pleasant and happy. When the relationship is very different and the external environment constrains and restricts any expression of the internal, then we have feelings that are disturbed and unhappy. The winner/loser world creates such a hostile environment that we are constantly responding with messages of emotional pain, unhappiness, discontentment and, after a time, depression.

Our biggest problem, as human beings, is that we are still evolving and many of the wonderful advances in our biology, and especially our brain, have some unpleasant side effects that have yet to be resolved. I am astounded how the extraordinary mental development that allows the average 4-6-year-old to appreciate their Theory of Mind (or as Ramachandran calls it the theory of other peoples' minds) also marks the introduction of lying – "I didn't do it! It was the dog." With their new ability to realise that they have a unique view of the world and that other people may not know what they know is an extraordinary breakthrough in perception that introduces us to the extraordinary world of the inner self and the magnificence of our imagination.

But the blessing of the imagination can be a burden, too. We now know that we can alter the functioning of the body through biofeedback. We can also anticipate the future, but if we anticipate poorly we can manifest fearfulness and dark displeasures in our mind and this 'negative thinking' can manifest in our body. The neurotransmitters in our brain are involved in this process, which is only to be expected. They can be involved as cause, co-operator and/or responders to our state of being.
So what processes occur in the brain when we become depressed? This is where it gets truly fascinating. The following description is drawn largely from Joseph LeDoux in *Synaptic Self,* with support from others like Cozolino in *The Neuroscience of Psychotherapy* and Andrewes in *Neuropsychology: From Theory to Practice.*

LeDoux argues that the real action occurs in the synapses. There are some 10^{15} connections in the brain from a base collection of 100 billion neurons. (This is equivalent to 1/5th of the estimated number of particles in the universe!) If only we were able to hit specific neurons and synapses then we might well have a 'magic bullet' cure. Still, we have been able to discover that there are some neurotransmitters (and/or neuromodulators) that can affect limited areas of the brain. The most widespread neurotransmitters are the excitory glutamate and the inhibitive GABA, but the discovery of the monoamine neurotransmitters - serotonin, dopamine, epinephrine (adrenalin) and norepinephrine (noradrenalin) has allowed for a more specific treatment of depressive symptoms.

Serotonin has been targeted because it seems to have relevance to positive mood. Certainly the other monoamines have their specific relevance, but we will leave their story for another time and concentrate on the nature of serotonin. What is really going on up there in the synapses? The next few paragraphs may be a bit technical, but I urge you to persevere even if you only get the overall idea. I am often frustrated by books that don't give the technical detail, so for those that are interested, let's see what happens in our brain.

The most common underlying cause of depression is prolonged stress. Stress can come from many sources. Some level of short term stress can be helpful. It is beneficial for us to experience some stress because it acts to motivate us into positive action. We are not, however, designed for long-term stress or stress from abstract pressure. We are not designed for not being pretty enough or not having enough possessions or having to pay taxes. Under stress the adrenal cortex secretes cortisol in order to prepare the body to defend itself from a clear and present danger. This is the sympathetic nervous system, but the story is much more complex than this.

The amygdala, which is in the limbic region and responds to situations that promote fear, responds to stress and excites neurons in the hypothalamus to release CRF (corticotrophin-releasing factor) into the pituitary gland, which releases ACTH (adrenocorticotrophin hormone), which travels through the bloodstream to the adrenal cortex causing an increased secretion of cortisol. This is called the hypothalamus-pituitary-adrenal axis. Amongst the many areas of the body that are affected by cortisol, it also attaches to receptors in the hippocampus.

The hippocampus is important in the processing of new information, learning and the accessing of memories. During the period of stress the hippocampus shuts down. When a suitable number of receptors are occupied in the hippocampus it tells the hypothalamus to stop producing CRF and, so, the system regulates. We are designed to be mobilised for short periods, for the brief time of being under attack, but as Robert Sapolsky suggests, not for a thirty year mortgage!

Prolonged stress can damage the hippocampus, actually causing neuron death. As the hippocampus is concerned with explicit or declarative memory, stress can compromise thinking. Cell shrinkage and death can occur in the CA_3 region, but the worst affect is in the dentate gyrus. This is the part of the brain where learning occurs through the process of neurogenesis – the growth of new neurons. Neurogenesis increases when learning occurs and decreases when stress occurs. This is probably why stressed people often have a smaller hippocampus, but what is more important is that their neural system is in a severely disadvantaged state for learning. When you are stressed it is hard to learn and remember. It is also hard to recall. You are like a 'dead duck', but the body doesn't need you to be smart when being attacked by the sabre-tooth tiger. The body just wants you to fight. The trouble is that the winner/loser world doesn't give you anything to fight – except maybe your partner or your children or the driver that cut you off at the lights.

The hypothalamic-pituitary-adrenal axis (HPA axis) was not designed to give us long-term depression, but to help us deal with danger and difficulty in order to survive. Our stressful winner/loser culture is outside of the natural set-up of the body.

Without some alteration of the thinking that leads us to interpret day-to-day life as stressful, we are disadvantaged. In psychotherapy we try to alter beliefs to remove the stressful interpretation of life, but if the mind is badly affected by stress and the mind is unable to learn or process new information then we have a catch-22 dilemma.

Antidepressant treatment can have a positive effect in breaking the destructive cycle of CA_3 death and dentate gyrus loss of cell growth. This is achieved by the excitory effect of serotonin on GABA, which has an inhibitory effect on neuronal action potential in the amygdala. This calms the activity of the HPA axis. When the synapses of the hippocampus become prepared for explicit learning, due to the sense of reduced stress induced by anti-depressant treatment, it is possible for many of the psychotherapy methods to be more productive. There are a number of prescription products. We also have herbal products like St Johns Wort, which has some good evidence of positive effect. Then there are activities like meditation and other calming practices. Anything you might choose to add to your body needs to be thoroughly researched and recommended by experts. Like illness, depression is not a simple disorder, and can express itself differently in different people, so some adjustment of medication is not unusual.

The idea is to get the brain back into a learning state. What we don't want is for people to learn that you can pop a pill and overcome the winner/loser world. It is only by practice and participation that we learn new ways and break out of the winner/loser cycle. The most important thing is to connect with others. This can be just to smile at people as you walk down the street. It might be connecting with family members you have lost touch with. It might be volunteering for community work or just be being nicer to your workmates, even if they aren't so nice to you. It might be anything, but it needs to be something.

And now, the last parable.

● THE PARABLE OF THE FLOOD ●

Jack was a jovial man. He didn't have a worry in the world and had little hesitation in telling people this very fact. "I am a man who is blessed by the Lord. Nothing bad will ever happen to me. Why on earth would I worry?"

And it certainly worked for him. He had great friends and they all considered that Jack lived a great life. Then came the great rains of '92. No one had ever seen rain like it and it was pretty obvious that the river was going to flood. And so it did.

Just before the river broke its banks, Jack's neighbour drove up in his 4-wheel drive. "Come on Jack. We've got to go. The river is about to let loose!" Jack came out on the veranda and gave a big wave, "Don't worry Dan, the Lord is looking after me. You get yourself out of here, but I'll be just fine." Dan didn't like it, but he left Jack waving on the veranda.

The river burst its banks and the water quickly swept through the town. It wasn't long before the water was over the veranda and into the house. Jack climbed the stairs to the bedroom level and settled down to a good book. He was disturbed by his other neighbour calling outside the window. Jack lifted the window to see his good friend Peter in small boat. The boat was almost full. There was old Mrs Johnson and her cat, the young lass who recently moved in down the street with her two little children and a very wet Mr Bongo, the long-haired sheep dog, laying on the floor of the boat like a disgruntled mop. "Hey there Peter. That's a pretty full boat you've got there. I wouldn't want to cause you any trouble. You get these good people to dry land. I'll be just fine. The Lord is looking down on me today!"

Peter protested, but to no avail, so, he turned the boat around and wished Jack the best.

Jack got back to his book and just when the story was getting particularly exciting, the water came up over the stairs and lapped at his feet. But Jack wasn't worried. He took the book and climbed up through the attic and onto the roof. The rain had eased quite a bit and the view was quite extraordinary. Jack heard the sound of an engine behind him. He turned to see a helicopter heading his way. "Whatever will happen next?" Jack mumbled to himself.

The man inside used a megaphone to call down to him, "We've come to get you. I'll let down a ladder and you can climb up." Jack truly wondered what all the fuss was about. The Lord would look after him. For the third time he waved away the help of his friends and sat down quietly on the roof waiting for the Lord to save him.

The floodwater continued to rise. Although the rain had stopped where Jack lived, there was plenty of rain still falling up-river, which was making the flood worse. In the end, it was inevitable: Jack drowned.

The next thing he knew he was at the Pearly Gates being welcomed by St Peter into heaven. But Jack wasn't at all pleased, "What happened? Why didn't the Lord save me?" He was absolutely incredulous.

St Peter also seemed to be quite baffled. "I don't know what you mean, Jack. We sent you a 4-wheel drive, a boat and even a helicopter! What did you expect?" Jack learnt a valuable lesson that day, unfortunately just a little late.

◆ ◆ ◆ ◆ ◆ ◆ ◆ ◆ ◆ ◆

And the moral of the story? It is not what is created *for* us that will save us from the problems of the world, but what we create *with* what is made available to us. The winner/loser world separates us from the process of interaction, whereas the creative world invites us to participate in the experience.

♦♦♦ THE LAST WORD ♦♦♦

It is hard to believe that this is where we must leave our conversation. I hope your responses are scribbled throughout these pages, on napkins, beer coasters and etched into your mind. Again, I invite you to share your thoughts through the website, email, or post. But don't restrict your conversation to just me. Expose your ideas to friends and family and all those that encourage an open mind. I hope that number grows every day. Please look into the books I have listed as reference. I have included many of the books from my library that I have really enjoyed reading and have used as reference material for this book. In the Appendix I give a set of stories and examples that you can use to help develop your creative world skills. They can act as case studies for discussion groups or examples you can use to show others the creative world way.

Although this portal comes to a close I am excited by the prospect of possibly meeting you in person one day (dopamine rushing all over the place). Thank you so much for reading this book.

APPENDIX

♦♦♦ TRUE STORIES ♦♦♦

The following stories come from my personal experience. Some are altered to maintain privacy, but the essence of each story is here. Please read these stories and think about how *you* might react, how you might help, what you might do.

These are good case studies to practice the application of the 6 Practices. You might like to use them as examples in a discussion group. The 8 Differences and the 7 Demons are everywhere you look. These stories provide a neutral ground from which you can look at the winner/loser world and also begin to apply the creative world way to your own life.

What can you create?

KATE

Kate believed she had a spiritual connection to people who had passed on, and to the greater wisdom in the 'other world'. Her family, and particularly her husband, not only thought she was wrong, but also stupid to believe those things. On top of this, Kate's husband was constantly accusing her of being too soft and giving. In her family, women were expected to be a bit stupid, and that they should just get on with doing what they were supposed to do and not have annoying beliefs.

So, Kate feels awful about herself. It all seems so unfair, but is that because she is ungrateful or disrespectful? She feels awful again. Whenever she talks about what she believes, her family is critical. She defends herself and tries to get them to understand, but they never do and she feels awful again. She feels isolated and disconnected. She feels like an absolute loser. Yet, she knows that her beliefs are good and no matter what anyone says, she knows they are important. Still, this leaves her feeling awful, too.

One day she was driving with her husband to the local mall for some coffee. While they were stopped at a set of traffic lights, a window-washer tapped on her window. She looked at him and saw a fellow trying to get on, trying to look after himself. The windscreen was a bit dirty, she thought to herself, so she beckoned him to go ahead and clean the windscreen. It cost $2.

Immediately her husband rebuked her. "Why are you such a soft touch? We don't have money to give to just anyone on the street?" His reprimand was based on his frustration - he didn't go to work every day for her to waste his money on street people. She felt awful, but she also felt obligated to her husband. So she told him that when they were in the café she would not have a cup of coffee, just water. That would compensate for the payment to the man.

He grumbled a bit more, and she drove to the mall continuing to feel awful, but pleased to have stood up for herself. When they arrived at the café he ordered a coffee and a water. Her humiliation was complete. She drank her water without any sign of her disappointment. That was the only way she could win. She won by being defeated with grace. He won, too, but is this really one of those elusive win/win outcomes? I don't think so.

I asked her how she felt now, which was some days after. She was still upset. She wanted me to tell her that he was wrong. She wanted me to tell her that her beliefs are true. She wanted me to tell her that it could change and be better for her. Perhaps I could have told her all those things, but it wouldn't have helped, or at least, not for long.

We talked about the winner/loser world and her eyes lit up. Suddenly she could see that there was no *need* to convince *anyone* that her beliefs were true. All that mattered was that they were true for her. Her husband's attitude about her and the windscreen washer was not about her, it was about him. She realised how much this was telling her about her husband and her family. I wondered what she would create with that.

For the first time in a long time she felt comfortable about her ideas and beliefs, not because anyone agreed with her, but because she was able to accept that these beliefs were a part of her self-expression.

BOB

Bob went to work every day, and got told off every day. Someone was always telling him what to do or how to do it. Day after day, he came home tired and frustrated. What greeted him at home? On the best day his wife wanted to hug him and the kids wanted to play, but all he could cope with was some time-out. He needed peace and quiet with no demands and a little time to relax. Watching the TV and having a beer or two worked well. On the worst day he came home *wanting* a hug from his wife and to play with the kids, but they all ignored him because they had learnt that he needed his time-out and they had learnt how to cut off.

PETER

Peter would often say that he had no friends at school. He didn't feel confident enough to play team sports. He had no real friends to talk to and muck about with. His father tried to motivate him by telling him that he would never be any good until he got off his behind and did something. Peter didn't know how to do that any better than he was already trying to do, so he figured he would never be any good and so, why bother? They lived near the ocean and he used to like walking up by the cliffs. The view was great and the sound of the waves constantly punishing the rocks below showed real determination. Not like him. One day he jumped off. He probably thought that no one would really care. More than 350 people came to his funeral. He had never felt connection with any of them.

GREG

Greg was keen, enthusiastic and talented. His acting career was going well and being cast in a new production was a great thrill. The play was being performed for the first time and suggestions were invited from the start of rehearsals. Greg worked hard and would give suggestions that he really believed would improve the play. Almost every suggestion was summarily dismissed. A number of times someone would make a similar suggestion and the director would accept it. Greg just tried harder, but his suggestions began to be delivered with a tone of sarcasm. Finally a cast-mate took him aside because he couldn't stand it anymore. "Listen Greg, I'm sick of this. Can't you see what is going on? You're the tallest bloke in the cast and look how short he is." Greg looked and he could see that was true. "He always picks on the tallest guy. So, just shut up and put up with it. It's happened to me, so just shut up. Okay?" Greg got the point and rehearsals were much less stressful. On opening night the director came backstage after the show. He heaped praise on everyone and finally turned to Greg. In a questioning and bemused tone he simply commented, "Well, my daughter thought you were good." Nothing had changed.

DANNY

When Danny met John, the new guy at work, he found him to be quite a nice fellow. He was friendly and easygoing. Danny thought that John was a breath of fresh air in the place. Over time though Danny found John was annoying. John was so positive and confident. He was never afraid to speak up and the way he said things didn't seem to bother anyone anyway. He was a real team player and helped Danny a number of times without trying to take the credit or show off. But Danny couldn't help feeling bad about John. John was everything the company wanted in a manager and he was a threat to Danny's chance of promotion. Danny found himself so preoccupied with what John was doing that his performance at work began to slip. He even found that he was becoming testy at home, too.

There was no way that this was going to work out well for Danny. He just knew it. How do you compete with a guy that isn't trying to beat you? The more Danny tried to compete, the further behind he became. It's bad enough when your best is not good enough for others, but it is depressing when your best is not good enough at all.

PAUL

Paul's Mum was too busy. She was trying to raise three children on her own and had to work several jobs to make ends meet. Getting ahead was almost impossible, but Paul's bad behaviour at home and at school was destroying any chance she had. At home, Paul was abusive both physically and verbally. He and his Mum would frequently end up in a big fight, and sometimes she would lash out and hit him. He would just front up for more. It was breaking her heart, but there was no sign that anything would change. What Paul didn't say, probably because he didn't realise it himself, was that all he wanted was more attention from his Mum. She was so busy and had no time for him. If he was good and helped she would be nice, but only for a minute before she went to work again or went to sleep. When she was mad at him she would give him more time. When she hit him, it hurt, but at least they were connecting. It was the only way he could figure out how to get her attention. That is, without sharing his feelings, which he thought would only make his Mum feeling guilty and depressed. Everyone loses. In a battle there is rarely a winner, just the one that loses the least.

KATRINA

Katrina hated going out. When she met a new guy she would only give a small part of herself. If he seemed interested, she would sometimes pretend to be difficult. Often he would leave without asking her out again, but at least she avoided the emotional upset of being dumped or used. It was easiest to go with men that she didn't really like. That way it wouldn't matter when they broke up. She would often say, "I just keep going out with the same kind of useless guy. It's so predictable." Katrina was a real winner at being a loser. She knew how to make it feel like it was not her fault. She knew how not to be disappointed. She knew how to hold the high moral ground. She just didn't know how to be happy in the company of other people.

BETTY

Betty swiped the card through the eftpos machine, but it didn't work. The readout showed that the card had expired, but she could see that was not correct. She tried again. This time the machines failed to read the card at all. Without looking up she said, "I'm sorry" and swiped the card again. It failed again and she apologised again. Another salesperson came to help. This time the machine acknowledged the card, but the woman pressed the wrong button and the transaction stopped. Betty was forced to say again, "I'm sorry". The card was swiped again and, this time, everything worked and the machine was, at last, satisfied. Betty, on the other hand, was a mess. She muttered several more apologies and began to explain how stupid she was. Her shoulders slumped and her eyes glazed. She was a complete loser. She had failed the customer and her friend and the machine. I was the customer and I tried to point out to her that I was not worried and that you can't fail a machine. But the winner/loser world needed someone to be at fault and Betty seemed to be used to that position. The machine was smart. It didn't say anything, accepted no blame and only presented instruction. What chance did Betty have? I gave her a quick winner/loser world talk and she relaxed noticeably before saying, "Can you come with me everywhere?" I told her I would write a book instead, and she could take that with her.

And I have.

REFERENCE AND
FURTHER READING LIST

Neurobiology
Amen, D. 2001 *Healing ADHD* Berkley Books. New York
Andrews, D. 2001 *Neuropsychology: From theory to Practice* Psychology PressHove, UK
Carter, R. *Mapping the Mind* Phoenix, London
Cozolino, L. 2002 *The Neuroscience of Psychotherapy* Norton, New York
Damasio, A. 2000 *The Feeling of What Happens* Vintage, London
        2003 *Looking for Spinoza* Harcourt Books. London
        2004 *Descarte's Error* Penguin. New York
Edelman, G.M. 1992 *Bright Air, Brilliant Fire* Basic Books, New York
Goldberg, E. 2001 *The Executive Brain* Oxford University Press. UK
Greenfield, S. 1997 *The Human Brain* Weidenfeld & Nicholson. London
Hoffman, D. 1998 *Visual Intelligence* Norton. New York
Le Doux, J. 1996 *The Emotional Brain* Simon and Schuster. New York
        2002 *The Synaptic Self* Penguin, New York
Pinker, S. 1994 *The Language Instinct* William Morrow & Co. New York
        1997 *How the Mind Works* Norton. USA
Ramachandran, V.S. & Blakeslee, S. 1998 *Phantoms in the Brain* Fourth Estate. London
Rossi, E. 1993 *The Psychobiology of Mind & Body Healing* Norton. New York
        2002 *The Psychobiology of Gene expression* Norton. New York
Sapolsky, R. 2004 *Why Zebras Don't Get Ulcers, Third Ed* Henry Holt Publishers. New York
Siegel, D. 1999 *Developing Minds* The Guilford Press. New York
        2006 *The Mindful Brain in Psychotherapy* Norton. New York
Siegel, D. & Hartzell, M. 2003 *Parenting from the Inside out* Penguin. New York

Paleoanthropology / Biology
Bronowski, J. 1973 *The Ascent of Man* Little, Brown & Co., New York.
Davidson, I. & Noble, W. 1996 *Human Evolution Language and Mind* Cambridge University. UK
Dawkins, R. 1976 *The Selfish Gene* Oxford University Press. UK
        1986 *The Blind Watchmaker* Penguin. London
Deacon, T. 1997 *The Symbolic Species* Penguin Press London

Dunbar, R. 1996 *Grooming Gossip and the Evolution of Language* Faber & Faber London

Jurmain, T. et al 2001 *Essentials of Physical Anthropology* Wadsworth, USA.

Mithen, S. 1996 *The Prehistory of the Mind* Thames and Hudson. London

Philosophy

de Botton, A. 2004 *Status Anxiety* Pantheon Books. New York

Dali Lama 2005 *The Universe in a Single Atom* Morgan Road Books. USA

Goleman, D 1995 *Emotional Intelligence* Bloomsbury. London
      1995 *Vital Lies, Simple Truths* Bloomsbury. London

Hillman, J. 1975 *Revisioning psychology* HarperCollins. New York
      1995 *Kinds of Power* Currency Doubleday. New York
      1997 *The Soul's Code* Warner Books. USA

Horgan, J. 1999 *The Undiscovered Mind* Wiedenfeld& Nicholson. London

Houston, J. 1996 *The Mythic Life* Harper SanFrancisco. USA
      1997 *The Possible Human* Tarcher. USA
      1998 *A Passion for the Possible* Harper SanFrancisco. USA
      2004 *Jump Time* Sentient Publications. USA

Ridley, M. 1996 *The origins of Virtue* Viking. UK

Wilson, E.O. 1998 *Consilience. The Unity of Knowledge* Little Brown & Co. London

Cosmology

Hawking, S. 1993 *Black Holes, Baby Universes and Other Essays* BCA, New York.
      1996 *A Brief History of Time. 10th Anniversary Edition* Bantam Books. New York

Hawking, S. & Penrose, R. 1996 *The Nature of Space and Time* Princeton University Press. USA

Lederman, L. 1998 *The God Particle* Bantam Press. London

Psychotherapy

Glasser, W. 1965 *Reality Therapy* Harper and Rowe. New York
      1998 *Choice Therapy* HarperCollins. New York

Hillman, J. & Ventura, M. 1993 *We've had a hundred years of Psychotherapy and the World's Getting Worse* Harper San Francisco. USA

Johnson and Whiffen eds –2003 *Attachment Processes in Couple and Family Therapy.* The Guilford Press. New York

Seligman, M. 2002 *Authentic Happiness* The Free Press. New York

Consciousness
Blackmore, S. 1999 *The Meme Machine* Oxford University Press. UK
　　　2003 *Consciousness: An Introduction* Hodder & Stoughton. UK
Dennett, D. 1991 *Consciousness Explained* Penguin Books. London
　　　1996 *Kinds of Minds* Weidenfeld & Nicholson. London
Ramachandran, V.S. 2004 *A Brief Tour of Human Consciousness*
Pearsons. New York
Creativity
Buzan, T. 1993 *The Mindmap Book* BBC Books. UK
De Bono, E. 1990 *I am right You are Wrong* Viking. London
　　　1992 *Serious Creativity* HarperCollins. London
　　　1998 *Simplicity* Viking. London
　　　1999 *New Thinking for the New Millenium* Penguin. London
Magazines
New Scientist
Scientific American
Scientific American Mind